CONNECTING
WITH GOD

CONNECTING
WITH GOD

Prayers for Those Who
Have Yet to Find the Words

William J. O'Malley

ORBIS BOOKS
Maryknoll, New York 10545

Founded in 1970, Orbis Books endeavors to publish works that enlighten the mind, nourish the spirit, and challenge the conscience. The publishing arm of the Maryknoll Fathers and Brothers, Orbis seeks to explore the global dimensions of the Christian faith and mission, to invite dialogue with diverse cultures and religious traditions, and to serve the cause of reconciliation and peace. The books published reflect the views of their authors and do not represent the official position of the Maryknoll Society. To learn more about Maryknoll and Orbis Books, please visit our website at www.maryknollsociety.org.

Library of Congress Cataloging-in-Publication Data

O'Malley, William J.
    Connecting with God: prayers for those who have yet to find the words / William J. O'Malley.
        p. cm.
    ISBN 978-1-62698-011-2
    1. Prayers. 2. Prayer—Christianity I. Title
BV245.O43 2013
242'.802—dc23

                                                    2012032173

For
Michael Leach

For prayer is nothing else than being
on terms of friendship with God.

—SAINT TERESA OF AVILA

Contents

Introduction

The Latin root of "religion" is *religare*—"to bind tightly." So, genuine religion means a person-to-Person *connection* with God. Anyone can sit through endless rituals, initiations, hymns, and homilies, but if that *felt* linkage isn't there, there's no authentic religion.

Nor can God truly "prove" himself in textbooks, or logical outlines, or glutted chalkboards, or even lifelong head-trip discussions. God can prove himself only in exactly the way any other *person* can become trustworthy: first, being noticed, then seeming to merit some personal sharing, gradually developing mutual credibility, spending time and talk in the slow process of getting-to-know-you. Only then, as the trust slowly deepens, faith usually means going out on a limb together and *really* testing the relationship. You don't become true friends by going to the circus together but only by going through hell together. And remaining friends. Same with God. If you expect it to be instant gratification, sorry. Real friendship takes effort.

All the theology courses, homilies, and books can never be more than a warm up. Not welcome signs but arrows along the way. All the logical trails point toward some kind of necessary Mind-Behind-It-All, suggesting that searching for a personal connection with this God isn't futile, that there really *is* a Being, outside our minds, who validates the idea of a God that even atheists have. Faith is a *calculated risk*—both reasonable and beyond the reach of reason. Like love. Logical evidence and arguments for the existence of God could lead readers only to a strong degree of *probability* that God exists. At that point they might know *about* God. But they may not know *God*. Religion hasn't ignited yet.

Like matchmakers, all those secondhand words can merely make general suggestions about what might happen when the two persons–reader and God–get alone together.

That person-to-Person connection, then, is what this volume is intended to move forward, risking time alone together. But that's difficult with a relative stranger, as on a first date. So you go to someone more experienced and ask, "What am I gonna *say*? Give me a couple of starters, so I don't have to ask, 'Well, uh, what do you think about, like, the death penalty?'" These pages are conversation starters for anyone interested in giving God a chance to become a better friend.

Once you actually start to feel you're connecting to another Person, for heaven's sake (literally) dump the book and just feel at home together! Like a couple of friends in a long car trip, when the words have run out but the appreciation of being together is still real and precious.

Neither religious presentations nor religious education are religion. Praying is.

Ahem, uh, Hello?

Quiet my mind. Open my heart. Quicken my soul.

PRESENCE

> Great Friend,
> I trust you *have* been my Friend
> who gave me life
> and those I love
> and a purpose I'd like to understand.
> And so, from my side,
> I'd like to become a better friend.
> Amen.

GRACE

> Father, please help me know you, person-to-Person.

PSALM (ISAIAH 53:6–7)

> Up to now, we humans blundered about,
> bumping into things and one another
> like sheep in sore need of direction.
> Then God chose him to be the champion,
> to be the answer, to show us *how.*
> Into himself, he took it all—
> the lostness, the confusion, the stupidity, the
> sins—

paid all our outstanding debts for us.
He was battered about but never said a word,
a lamb picked out for slaughter.
And he never said a single word.

HYMN

Where am I? Who am I?
How did I come to be here?
What is this thing called the world?
How did I come into the world?
Why was I not consulted?
And if I am compelled to take part in it,
Where is the director?
I want to see him.

—SØREN KIERKEGAARD

READING

Those who believe that they believe in God, but without
passion in their hearts, without anguish in mind, without
uncertainty, without doubt, without an element of despair
even in consolation, believe in the God *idea*, not God himself.

—MIGUEL DE UNAMUNO

SCRIPTURE

The next day, John the Baptist was standing with two of
his disciples when he saw Jesus walking by. "See," he said.
"There he is. The Lamb of God." The two were intrigued and
set out after Jesus.

After a while, Jesus sensed them behind him and stopped.
"Can I help you? What are you looking for?"

They stammered a bit and said, "Rabbi, uh, where do you
live?"

Jesus smiled and said, "Come, and see."
So they did.

—JOHN 1:36–39

CLOSING

Great Friend,
I trust you are always ready
to be better known.
I'd like to be ready, too.
Amen.

Importance

Quiet my mind. Open my heart. Quicken my soul.

PRESENCE

> Great Friend,
> sometimes I feel
> like a blindfolded kid in a party game—
> turned round and round,
> disoriented, confused.
> Give me some reassurance, please?
> Amen.

GRACE

> Father, help me grasp in my inmost heart that
> it all makes sense.

PSALM 23

> My shepherd is the Lord. What more could
> I ask?
> We rest, two friends in a quiet meadow
> near a peaceful pool where he heals my soul.
> Even when I walk down shadowy paths,
> I'm not alone, so I'm not afraid
> because his hand is on my shoulder.
> He feeds my soul when I forget,
> firms up my spine when I feel like a fool.

4

He never questions what I deserve.
Yet how could he possibly care for me?

HYMN

Joy to the world, the Lord is come!
Let earth receive her King;
Let every heart prepare him room,
And heaven and nature sing,
And heaven and nature sing,
And heaven, and heaven, and nature sing.
Joy to the world, the Savior reigns!
Let men their songs employ;
While fields and floods, rocks, hills, and
    plains
Repeat the sounding joy,
Repeat the sounding joy,
Repeat, repeat, the sounding joy.
He rules the world with truth and grace,
And makes the nations prove
The glories of his righteousness,
And wonders of his love,
And wonders of his love,
And wonders, wonders, of his love.

—Isaac Watts

READING

One day an African boy, wandering in the forest, suddenly stopped, spellbound by a bird trilling somewhere overhead. The melody soared and swooped and cascaded, as if the soul of the bird were winging from her throat. And then there she was, perched on a branch above his head, resplendent in feathers of blood red and iridescent blue. She cocked a quizzical eye at him and fluttered down to his bare shoulder, grasping it gently in her silver talons.

Gleefully the boy ran home with his prize, bursting into the hut just as his father returned, grim and empty-handed from the hunt. "Father," the boy cried, "look what I found! Isn't she beautiful? What shall we feed her?"

"Feed *her*?" his father growled. "What shall we feed your brothers and sisters? There is *nothing*!"

The father grasped the bird from the boy's shoulder and strangled its cries. "Now," he said darkly, "we can live one more day."

But in killing the bird, he had killed the song. And in killing the song, he had killed himself.

SCRIPTURE

Jesus said to his friends, "You are in such a fuss about yourselves! Worrying about what you eat and what people think about your body or what you wear on it. Isn't being alive more important than the food that keeps it going? Isn't having a heartbeat more important than what encases it? Think about the birds of the air. They don't let themselves worry about when to plant and when to harvest. They have no storehouses or barns, yet God somehow makes sure they're taken care of. Don't you realize you are far more important than birds? Will any of your fretting guarantee you'll wake up one more day? Will you just pause for a single moment and figure out for yourself what is *really* important?"

—LUKE 12:22–26

CLOSING

Great Friend,
it's so hard to accept
that someone like me
could be important
to someone like you.
Help my disbelief.
Amen.

Confidence

Quiet my mind. Open my heart. Quicken my soul.

PRESENCE

Great Friend,
everywhere I turn
they hold up mirrors:
"You'll never be like . . . " and "See the
   flaws!"
and "We're a bit disappointed."
Rescue me
into some kind of sanity
and peace.
Amen.

GRACE

Father, help me make the best self I can from
   what I have.

PSALM

Don't let your sense of worth depend
on how much you make or what you *seem*
   to be.
Hasn't the God who sees all truly said,
"I could never abandon you! Not ever!"
Uplifted by that love, why can't you say,

7

"The Lord is with me. I will not be afraid!
Who could make him stand aside?"

—HEBREWS 13:5–6

HYMN

I am what I am.
I am my own special creation.
So, come take a look,
Give me the hook or an ovation.
It's my world
that I want to take a little pride in—
my world, and it's
not a place I have to hide in.
Life's not worth a damn,
'til you can say, "Hey, world,
I am what I am."

—JERRY HERMAN[1]

READING

We who lived in concentration camps can remember the
men who walked through the huts comforting others, giving
away their last piece of bread. They may have been few in
number, but they offer sufficient proof that everything can
be taken from a man but one thing: the last of the human
freedoms—to choose one's attitude in any given set of circum-
stances, to choose one's own way.

—VIKTOR FRANKL

SCRIPTURE

Jesus said to his friends, "If you want to come along with
me, don't let your worries about yourself get in your own

---

[1] "I Am What I Am." May 9, 2008. Used by permission of the Hal
Leonard Corporation, 7777 West Bluemound Road, P.O. Box 13819,
Milwaukee, WI 53213.

way. Pick up my burden with me, and come along. If you're worried about what you're risking, what you might lose, you'll die without ever having known what living was for! What reward would be huge enough if it meant surrendering all claim to your soul, your self, your freedom to be you? Nothing! If you lose possession of your own self, what do you have left that's worth having?"

—MATTHEW 16:24–26

CLOSING

> Great Friend,
> remind me always that
> no one degrades me
> unless I permit it.
> Help me trust
> your confidence in me.
> Amen.

Patience

Quiet my mind. Open my heart. Quicken my soul.

PRESENCE

> Great Friend,
> something dumb and mutinous in me
> despises waiting, wants to *zoom*,
> to trample past the boring delays,
> the "only when we're ready's" and the "not
>   just yet's."
> But defying you cripples me.
> Amen.

GRACE

> Father, make the fool in me accept what can't
>   be changed.

PSALM

> The Lord gives us what time we have.
> Then, friend, let the Lord judge how long
>   things take.
> The farmers know how to wait on God,
> that God controls the rains, not they.
> So, you, be content to grow as God wills.
> All the prophets learned persistence,

knew nothing can live that evolves over-
night.
How long did Abraham wait for Isaac?
How long did Job have to wait and trust?
In patience you shall possess your soul.

—JAMES 5:7–11

HYMN

A noiseless, patient spider
I mark'd where on a little promontory it
stood isolated,
Mark'd how to explore the vacant vast sur-
rounding,
It launch'd forth filament, filament, filament,
out of itself,
Ever unreeling them, ever tirelessly speeding
them.
And you, O my soul where you stand,
Surrounded, detached, in measureless oceans
of space,
Ceaselessly musing, venturing, throwing,
seeking the spheres to connect them,
Till the bridge you will need be form'd,
till the ductile anchor hold,
Till the gossamer thread you fling catch somewhere, O my soul.

—WALT WHITMAN

READING

I remember one morning when I discovered a cocoon in
the back of a tree just as a butterfly was making a hole in its
case and preparing to come out. I waited a while, but it was
too long appearing and I was impatient. I bent over it and
breathed on it to warm it. I warmed it as quickly as I could,

and the miracle began to happen before my eyes, faster than life. The case opened; the butterfly started slowly crawling out. And I shall never forget my horror when I saw how its wings were folded back and crumpled; the wretched butterfly tried with its whole trembling body to unfold them. Bending over it, I tried to help it with my breath, in vain. It needed to be hatched out patiently, and the unfolding of the wings should be a gradual process in the sun. Now it was too late. My breath had forced the butterfly to appear all crumpled, before its time. It struggled desperately and, a few seconds later, died in the palm of my hand.

That little body is, I do believe, the greatest weight I have on my conscience. For I realize today that it is a mortal sin to violate the great laws of nature. We should not hurry, we should not be impatient, but we should confidently obey the external rhythm.

—NIKOS KAZANTZAKIS

SCRIPTURE

"This is what the parable means. The seed the sower strewed is God's invitation. The path means hardened people with no real depth, who let the word of God graze them. But the winds that whirl the world whisk it away. Some seed falls on rocky hearts, too, but they can absorb nothing, and the sun dries the life from the message. Some seed does take shallow root among tough briars that allow it to grow just long enough to be choked. But when the word falls into a willing soul, it's held fast by an honest heart and, with patient persistence, bears bountiful fruit in God's good time."

—LUKE 8:11–15

CLOSING

Great Friend,
help me understand

why Jesus chose to rise to his challenge
only one slow step at a time.
Amen.

A Single Seed

PRESENCE

> Great Friend,
> the need for healing
> is so vast it's discouraging.
> Something strong inside me
> wants to belittle my power.
> Amen.

GRACE

> Father, remind me that a single seed can start
> a forest.

PSALM

> The Lord of Hosts spoke to Jeremiah,
> "Before you were a flicker of life in the
> womb,
> I knew the very core of you.
> I loved you, chose you, consecrated you to
> me."
> Then I stammered, "L-lord G-god! No!
> I'm no speaker. And I am f-f-far too y-young!"
> The voice of the Lord was soft and harsh:
> "Do *not* say, 'I am too young'!

14

You will go to those I show to you
And soften their resistance and indifference.
Don't be afraid. I will be with you.
I will transform your weakness into power."

—JEREMIAH 1:4–8

HYMN

I am only one,
But still I am one.
I cannot do everything,
But still I can do something;
And because I cannot do everything
I will not refuse to do the something that I
can do.

—EDWARD EVERETT HALE

READING

From numberless diverse acts of courage and belief, human history is shaped. Each time a man stands for an ideal, or acts to improve the lot of others, or strikes out against injustice, he sends forth a tiny ripple of hope, and crossing each other from a million different centers of energy and daring, those ripples build a current that can sweep down the mightiest walls of oppression.

—ROBERT F. KENNEDY

SCRIPTURE

"You! No, don't turn around. *You!* You are the salt of the earth. If you offer no zest to the lives you touch, what a tasteless world! What a wasted life! You are the light I send to ignite the world! It takes only one tiny spark to do it. And once it's burning, don't dream of hiding it away. Your light is to help people find their way to livelier lives. That's what you're *for*. So that your life makes them thank God *they're* alive, and their aliveness *is* the glory of God."

—MATTHEW 5:13–16

CLOSING

> Great Friend,
> I believe you made a universe from nothing,
> that you used mud and spit to work miracles.
> Help me to grasp
> that I am not as unpromising
> as I seem.
> Amen.

Alchemy

Quiet my mind. Open my heart. Quicken my soul.

PRESENCE

> Great Friend,
> peculiar medieval alchemists set themselves
> to transform lead into gold.
> Sometimes I really wonder—
> after what you've done to me—
> if you haven't set me the same task.
> Amen.

GRACE

> Father, remind me my power comes from get-
> ting out of your way.

PSALM

> How could I look at a handicap as a gift?
> So three times I begged God to uproot mine.
> But he refused and said, "I'm all you need!
> My power finds fulfillment *through* your
> weakness."
> If that's what God wants, that works for me.
> My weakness opens me to God.
> Let him fill my empty pockets with his power.
> I can accept myself now, flaws and all,

and sudden setbacks show me who I am.
Imperfections? Bad luck? Let Christ take
  them over.
The weaker I am, the more God strengthens
  me!

—2 CORINTHIANS 12:8–10

HYMN

When I compare
What I have lost with what I have gained
What I have missed with what attained,
Little room do I find for pride,
  I am aware.
How many days have been idly spent;
How like an arrow the good intent
Has fallen short or been turned aside.
  But who shall dare
To measure loss and gain in this wise?
Defeat may be victory in disguise;
The lowest ebb is the turn of the tide.

—HENRY WADSWORTH LONGFELLOW

READING

The truth is that our finest moments are most likely to oc-
cur when we are feeling deeply uncomfortable, unhappy, or
unfulfilled. For it is only in such moments, propelled by our
discomfort, that we are likely to step out of our ruts and start
searching for different ways or truer answers.

—M. SCOTT PECK

SCRIPTURE

"Master," Simon sighed, "we've worked hard all night
long and come back empty-handed. But if you want me to,
I'll drop over the nets again." So they did, and all at once the

lake was thrashing silver with fish. Simon and his brother, Andrew, hauled in so many fish that their nets were ready to break, and they called their mates in the other boat to come and help. And both boats were so filled with fish the water was splashing over the gunnels. Simon and his partners, James and John, stood dumbfounded, up to their hips in heaving mounds of fish.

Simon fell to his knees and hung his head, rocking in disbelief. "Master, please. You're too much for me. I can't take this. Leave me. I'm a sinful man."

But Jesus said to him quietly. "Enough of your fears and your flaws. Come with me, and I will have you catching souls!"

—LUKE 5:5–10

CLOSING

> Great Friend,
> the deepest question
> is not What can I do for you?
> but
> What can you do with me?
> Amen.

Character

Quiet my mind. Open my heart. Quicken my soul.

PRESENCE

> Great Friend,
> from the challenges you send,
> help me forge
> a deep leaden keel.
> Amen.

GRACE

> Father, remind me you gave me a mind of my
> own for a reason.

PSALM

> I fall to my knees before our Father
> from whom we discern what *father* means:
> the one who ignited life for us,
> whose love sustains and challenges us.
> I beg him to empower you with his Spirit,
> to strengthen not your bodies but your souls.
> Open the doors of your self and welcome
> him,
> so that, rooted deeply and firmly in love,
> together with all those God cherishes,
> you might grasp with all your heart and soul

the boundless dimensions of Christ's love!
It is beyond the meaning of length or breadth
or height or depth. Limitless as God.
Open yourself—and be filled beyond fullness!
—EPHESIANS 3:14–19

HYMN

One ship sails East,
And another West,
By the self-same winds that blow,
'Tis the set of the sails
And not the gales,
That tells the way we go.

Like the winds of the sea
Are the waves of time,
As we journey along through life,
'Tis the set of the soul,
That determines the goal,
And not the calm or the strife.
—ELLA WHEELER WILCOX

READING

I look forward confidently to the day when all who work for a living will be one, with no thought to their separateness as Negroes, Jews, Italians or any other distinctions. This will be the day when we bring into full realization the American dream—a dream yet unfulfilled. A dream of equality of opportunity, of privilege and property widely distributed; a dream of a land where men will not take necessities from the many to give luxuries to the few; a dream of a land where men will not argue that the color of a man's skin determines the content of his character; a dream of a nation where all our gifts and resources are held not for ourselves alone, but as instruments of service for the rest of humanity; the dream

of a country where every man will respect the dignity and
worth of the human personality.

—MARTIN LUTHER KING, JR.

SCRIPTURE

"Be wary of flashy swindlers with seductive easy answers.
They come up to you, seeming as harmless as sheep, but check
their teeth. Don't judge by charm but by reliability, not by
what they claim, but by what they produce. You can't get life
from a stone, or compassion from a snake, or lasting happiness from a moment's thrill. A genuine heart produces sincere
kindness, but the offerings of a wicked heart slowly decay into
bitterness, betrayal, acid. In the end you see that what comes
from the mouth arises from whatever really fills the heart."

—MATTHEW 7:15–20; LUKE 6:43–44

CLOSING

Great Friend,
"shrewd as serpents
but harmless as doves"
is nowhere near as simple
as it sounds.
Amen.

Daring

Quiet my mind. Open my heart. Quicken my soul.

PRESENCE

> Great Friend,
> let me grasp
> that life is too short
> to be small.
> Amen.

GRACE

> Father, help me be as sure as I pretend to be.

PSALM

> I know now how to keep going when I have
>   nothing
> just as well as when I have more than enough.
> The secret is to face the situation I find
> rather than moan about all that I'm missing.
> Filled or empty, plenty or famine,
> I'm ready to take whatever God sends.
> I'll face anything with the One who strength-
>   ens me.
> My confidence comes from God's confidence
>   in me.
>
> —PHILIPPIANS 4:12–13

HYMN

How dull it is to pause, to make an end,
To rust unburnished, not to shine in use!
As though to breathe were life. Life piled on
    life
Were all too little, and of one to me
Little remains; but every hour is saved
From that eternal silence, something more,
A bringer of new things; and vile it were
For some three suns to store and hoard my-
    self,
And this gray spirit yearning in desire
To follow knowledge like a sinking star,
Beyond the utmost bound of human thought.

—ALFRED, LORD TENNYSON

READING

It is not the critic who counts, not the man who points out how the strong man stumbled, or where the doer of deeds could have done better. The credit belongs to the man who is actually in the arena, whose face is marred by dust and sweat and blood, who strives valiantly, who errs and comes short again and again, who knows the great enthusiasms, the great devotions, and spends himself in a worthy cause, who at best knows achievement and who at the worst if he fails at least fails while daring greatly, so that his place shall never be with those cold and timid souls who know neither victory nor defeat.

—THEODORE ROOSEVELT

SCRIPTURE

In the darkest hours before dawn, Jesus came walking across the water, through the raging waves, toward their boat.

His friends were scared mindless, muttering, "It's a ghost," and whimpering in terror.

But Jesus called out quickly, "Courage! It's only me! Don't be afraid!"

Then Peter, with his usual bravado, called back, "Master, if it really is you, call me to come out to you on the water!"

Even through the flashes of spray, they could see Jesus smile. "Come."

So Peter boldly leaped over the side and started walking toward Jesus on the troughs and crests of the waves. But suddenly, gaping down at the wild waters, he recovered his wits enough to lose his nerve, and he began to sink.

"O Lord," he cried, "save me!"

Jesus' hand flashed out and caught him, holding him safe. "Oh, how little you trust what I can do with you," he said. "Why did you trust yourself instead of me?"

The two of them climbed into the boat, and the wind fell calm. The men, who had seen it all, murmured, "Yes, yes, he is the son of God."

—MATTHEW 14:25–33

CLOSING

> Great Friend,
> if you intend
> any water-walking for me,
> let me feel your firm grasp
> sometime before my first step.
> Amen.

Anger

Quiet my mind. Open my heart. Quicken my soul.

PRESENCE

> Great Friend,
> I want to accept
> that my resentments
> frazzle only me.
> Amen.

GRACE

> Father, cure my touchy short-sightedness.

PSALM

> Didn't you learn, "Don't hit back"?
> One wrong doesn't justify another.
> Try your very best to live in peace.
> Revenge is God's prerogative, not yours.
> Instead, drive your enemies crazy
> by giving kindness back instead!
> Nastiness is just what they're expecting.
> So, if they're hungry, give them food.
> If they're thirsty, offer them a drink.
> You'll fry their brains! "What's this *about*?"
> You'll actually make them think!
> Kindness makes evil impotent.
>
> —ROMANS 12:17–21

26

HYMN

My Lord Supreme,
One thing I know for sure:
I can be truly happy
Only when you replace my anger
With forgiveness,
Then with compassion
And finally with oneness.

—SRI CHINMOY[2]

READING

Of the Seven Deadly Sins, anger is possibly the most fun. To lick your wounds, to smack your lips over grievances long past, to roll over your tongue the prospect of bitter confrontations still to come, to savor to the last toothsome morsel both the pain you are given and the pain you are giving back—in many ways it is a feast fit for a king. The chief drawback is that what you are wolfing down is yourself. The skeleton at the feast is you.

—FREDERICK BUECHNER

SCRIPTURE

"Wise men of every time and place have said, 'Do not murder.' But I'm telling you that anyone who lashes out in anger at a brother or sister is just as bad. To call a brother 'Idiot!' sets you up as his judge. And who are you to call your sister 'Loser!' You're tempting judgment yourself with that. Don't your own soul-scars remind you how disfiguring words can be? So if you open yourself to God in prayer, and suddenly you remember a grudge, stop right there. Get up, call the one

---

[2] Sri Chinmoy, *Ten Thousand Flower-Flames*, Part 89. Used by permission from Sri Chinmoy Centre.

you share the grudge with, and make peace. Only then will
you be able to deal honestly with God."

—MATTHEW 5:21–24

CLOSING

> Great Friend,
> inflict on me the profound wisdom
> of counting to ten.
> Amen.

False Gods

Quiet my mind. Open my heart. Quicken my soul.

PRESENCE

> Great Friend,
> so many voices
> want to tell me
> what it's all about.
> Hold on to my wandering attention.
> Amen.

GRACE

> Father, help me be cautious but not cowardly.

PSALM

> Who can believe how blind so many are?
> They plot and scheme, and God indulges
> them:
> Money, power, seductive glamour, fame.
> But then God says, "Enough, my friend. It's
> time,"
> And none of their toys can cheat the test of
> Death.
> And what does the lavish funeral celebrate?

How wasteful. Might as well have died at
    birth
for all they knew of what this life was for.
                            —ECCLESIASTES 6:1–6

HYMN

Thou shalt have one God only; who
Would be at the expense of two?
No graven images may be
Worshipped, except the currency:
Swear not at all; for, for thy curse
Thine enemy is none the worse:
At church on Sunday to attend
Will serve to keep the world thy friend:
Honour thy parents; that is, all
From whom advancement may befall:
Thou shalt not kill; but need'st not strive
Officiously to keep alive:
Do not adultery commit;
Advantage rarely comes of it:
Thou shalt not steal; an empty feat,
When 'tis so lucrative to cheat:
Bear not false witness; let the lie
Have time on its own wings to fly:
Thou shalt not covet, but tradition
Approves all forms of competition.
                            —ARTHUR HUGH CLOUGH

READING

A person will worship something, have no doubt about
that. We may think our tribute is paid in secret in the dark re-
cesses of our hearts, but it will out. That which dominates our
imaginations and our thoughts will determine our lives, and

our character. Therefore, it behooves us to be careful what we worship, for what we are worshiping we are becoming.

—RALPH WALDO EMERSON

SCRIPTURE

"Don't hoard away secret stashes and wads of money 'Just in case, just for me. Just for a rainy day.' Every minute you're not looking, the moths and rust are nibbling away at them, and some swindler is trying to figure a way to get at what's left. There are far more resilient riches, you know, valuables that simply can't be consumed or pinched or de-valued—not even by death. Don't you see? Whatever you call 'my treasure' *becomes* your heart and soul."

—MATTHEW 6:19–21

CLOSING

Great Friend,
You are the only One existing
worthy of worship.
Amen.

Making a Difference

Quiet my mind. Open my heart. Quicken my soul.

PRESENCE

> Great Friend.
> I'm here.
> Steady me
> when I stand up to be counted.
> Amen.

GRACE

> Father, help me see that true courage says, "I
> *can't!* . . . But I'll try."

PSALM

> How terrifying—to be grasped by the living
> God!
> Remember back when you first understood?
> You saw it would be a struggle to heed God's
> call,
> but you knew defeat was not a choice.
> One day they made fun of you, and then of
> your friends.
> But if you were *all* shut out, you joined
> hands,
> with a smile that kept your souls untouched.

Nothing "they" did could throw you then,
so how could "they" disturb you now?
Don't turn back! Keep your face to the Light!

—HEBREWS 10:31–39

HYMN

Shall I run and hide my fistful of stars,
Or try to harvest them all?
Shall I sit inside, secure by a hearth,
When the sky's on fire with their call?
Can a man abide the aching heart
To catch them up where they fall?
Just to sit and be, makes a no one of me,
When the gods make the wind blow fair.
And it matters not if I find the spot.
In the going, I'm already there.

When I stand and feel the wash of the rain
Draw paths out over the sea,
Then my heart goes stealing out to attain
Horizons I've never seen.
Shall I turn my heel, a man in vain,
When gods are calling to me?
Oh, the call may lie, but until I die,
I must go when the wind blows fair.
And it matters not if I find the spot.
In the going, I'm already there!

—WILLIAM O'MALLEY

READING

I have one life and one chance to make it count for something. . . . I'm free to choose what that something is, and the something I've chosen is my faith. Now, my faith goes beyond theology and religion and requires considerable work and effort. My faith demands—this is not optional—my faith demands I do whatever I can, wherever I am, whenever I can, for as long as I can with whatever I have, to try to make a difference.

—JIMMY CARTER

SCRIPTURE

The master came home and called his three servants to check on the money he'd entrusted to them when he left. The first said, "Sir, you gave me five thousand. Here's your investment in me and another five thousand I made with it." The master clapped him on the shoulder. "Fine!" he said. "You proved my trust in a fairly small challenge. Let's try you on something bigger. You're part of my staff now." The second returned the two thousand he'd received, plus two thousand more he'd earned with it. The master was just as pleased and rewarded him in the same way. The third servant edged forward timidly and said, "Sir, I know you're a tough bargainer. You seem to make a profit out of nearly nothing. So I took the thousand you gave me and buried it, safely, so you'd lose nothing because of my ignorance or carelessness or . . . whatever. Here it is back. Nothing lost." The master was furious. "Nothing lost except your future! What good are you? If you'd just put it in the bank, you'd have made *something*! Gutless! I'll show you tough. Give your wasted chance to the man with the ten. If you play it safe, you've lost before you've even begun. Out of my sight! Now!"

—MATTHEW 25:19–30

CLOSING

Great Friend,
your faith in me
sustains
my faith in you.
Amen.

Keeping Your Guard Up

Quiet my mind. Open my heart. Quicken my soul.

PRESENCE

> Great Friend,
> I'd like to learn
> what you taught the mindless oyster—
> how to change my irritations
> into pearls.
> Amen.

GRACE

> Father, help me see that my cautious defenses
> block you, too.

PSALM

> The Lord said to me, "Go watch the potter.
> He'll show what I want of you."
> So I went and watched him work his wheel,
> and whenever the piece was not quite right,
> he peeled it off without a word
> and whacked it back upon the wheel.
> And the Lord said, "I made you, yes?
> You're in my hands like the clay in the pot-
>   ter's.
> Does the potter ask the clay's permission

to wrench it into some new shape
the clay has no ability to fathom?
I don't intend you to be ordinary."
—JEREMIAH 18:1–8

HYMN

Look in the eyes of trouble with a smile,
Extend your hand and do not be afraid.
'Tis but a friend who comes to masquerade,
And test your faith and courage for awhile.
Fly, and he follows fast with threat and jeer.
Shrink, and he deals hard blow on stinging
    blow,
But bid him welcome as a friend, and lo!
The jest is off—the masque will disappear.
—ELLA WHEELER WILCOX

READING

The trouble with steeling yourself against the harshness of reality is that the same steel that secures your life against being destroyed secures your life also against being opened up and transformed by the holy power that life itself comes from. You can survive on your own. You can grow strong on your own. You can even prevail on your own. But you cannot become human on your own.

Surely that is why, in Jesus' sad joke, the rich man has as hard a time getting into Paradise as that camel through the needle's eye because with his credit card in his pocket, the rich man is so effective at getting for himself everything he needs that he does not see that what he needs more than anything else in the world can be had only as a gift. He does not see that the one thing a clenched fist cannot do is accept, even from *le bon Dieu* himself, a helping hand.
—FREDERICK BUECHNER

SCRIPTURE

Jacob sent his family and all his goods across the river, but he stayed behind, alone. As he lay in total darkness just before daybreak, a Stranger crept up and attacked him, wrestling with him, fall for fall, but could not defeat him. When the Stranger saw the false dawn and realized he could not subdue Jacob fairly, he hit him a hard crack on the hip and threw the leg out of joint. Still, Jacob held fast. "Let me *go*," the Stranger growled. "Daylight is almost here."

"I *won't*," Jacob huffed. "Unless you bless me!"

"What is your name?" the Stranger panted, maneuvering for advantage.

"Jacob," he answered.

"No more," the Stranger rasped. "Your name will be Israel—God-Wrestler—because you've grappled with God without giving up."

"And tell me *your* name," Jacob demanded.

"You want too much," the Stranger said, and instead he blessed Israel.

And as Jacob limped away, he knew he had wrestled with God and lived.

—GENESIS 32:22–30

CLOSING

Great Friend,
you offer so many challenges,
you surely can't mind
a few challenges in return.
Amen.

Questioning

Quiet my mind. Open my heart. Quicken my soul.

PRESENCE

> Great Friend,
> I want to understand and accept
> that you invite endless exploration
> but never conquest.
> Amen.

GRACE

> Father, give me patience—
> with ambiguity, incomplete answers,
> and your resistance to capture.

PSALM

> The Lord answered Job from the whirlwind:
> "Whose ignorance is this that challenges me?
> Where were you when I set the cosmos spin-
>   ning?
> Help me understand just how I did that.
> Were you there when all the stars shouted
>   together
> and the sons of morning sang for joy?
> Who called forth the seas, raging, from their
>   womb,

swaddled them in cloud, and gowned them
    in darkness?
Have you ever summoned the dawn, little
    Job,
and painted peaks and valleys with light?
I ask because you're so quick to question
how I dare make the choices for you that I
    do."

            —Job 38:1–15

HYMN

God moves in a mysterious way
His wonders to perform;
He plants His footsteps in the sea
And rides upon the storm.

   . . .

Blind unbelief is sure to err
And scan His work in vain;
God is His own interpreter,
And He will make it plain.

            —William Cowper

READING

Have patience with everything that remains unsolved in
your heart. Try to love the questions themselves, like locked
rooms and like books written in a foreign language. Do not
now look for the answers. They cannot now be given to you
because you could not live them. It is a question of experiencing everything. At present you need to *live* the question.
Perhaps you will gradually, without even noticing it, find
yourself experiencing the answer, some distant day.

            —Rainer Maria Rilke

SCRIPTURE

Paul stood up in front of the city council and said, "I see you Athenians take your religion seriously. As I walked through your city, I was intrigued by all your shrines, especially one that said, 'To an Unknown God.' And that is precisely the God I come to tell you about, the God you don't yet know, who made the world and everything in it, the God who spread out the heavens and the earth, who's too big for a single shrine to contain. This great God you revere without knowing has no need of our 'little offerings'—not when he is the one who gave us life and the breath to move! This is the God who created all the varied peoples in all the hidden-away corners of the world. He did that so that each of us could seek him out, groping through clues he's scattered all around. He will not be trapped, and yet he is as close to you as your own heartbeat. In him we live and move and root ourselves in existence. As one of your poets has said, 'All of us are this God's children.'"

—ACTS 17:22–28

CLOSING

Great Friend,
let me accept
that striving is more exciting—
and lasts a great deal longer—
than arriving.
Amen.

Uncertainty

Quiet my mind. Open my heart. Quicken my soul.

PRESENCE

> Great Friend,
> let me be content
> (for the moment)
> with what I can understand
> (for the moment).
> Amen.

GRACE

> Father, help me be comfortable with "pretty
> close."

PSALM

> The world accepts truth only when evi-
> dence—
> either hands-on or painstakingly quibbled—
> compels assent. God's wisdom eludes that!
> He delights in offering *Himself* as evidence,
> which worldlings can't fathom and sneer at
> as "stupid."
> Jews want miraculous "proof" and Greeks
> want ice-cold logic to obliterate doubt.
> So when we proclaim a Messiah, *crucified*,

Jews find it repulsive and Greeks irrational.
But for those willing to let God be God,
Christ is God's astonishing miracle *and* argu-
    ment.
Human certainties are straw compared to
    God's.
Human power is impotence next to God's
    "weakness."

—1 Corinthians 1:21–25

HYMN

Don't seek *too* much, good friend. We can-
    not say
what's yet in store for you or me.
Don't trust the stars to point your way.
Better to welcome whatever will be—
whether you soon will die, or stay
to watch the shore drink up the sea.
So quaff some wine as the moments flee!
Put small trust in posterity,
but trim your hopes—and grasp today.

—Horace (my translation)

READING

How is one to live a moral and compassionate existence when one is fully aware of the blood, the horror inherent in life, when one finds darkness not only in one's culture but within oneself? If there is a stage at which an individual life becomes truly adult, it must be when one grasps the irony in its unfolding and accepts responsibility for a life lived in the midst of such paradox. One must live in the middle of contradiction, because if all contradiction were eliminated at once, life would collapse. There are simply no answers to some of the great pressing questions. You continue to live them out, making your life a worthy expression of leaning into the light.

—Barry Lopez

SCRIPTURE

As they were walking along, Jesus asked his friends, "What do people say about who I am?" They dithered a bit. "Some say you're really John the Baptist. Others say you're, uh, the prophet Elijah come back to life. Or maybe Jeremiah."

"And what about you? What do you say?"

Not surprisingly, Simon Peter spoke up. "You're the Christ. You're the Son of the Living God." And he eyed the others, daring anyone to correct him.

"Good for you, Simon!" Jesus chuckled, clapping his meaty shoulder. "You didn't come to that from researching books or making calculations. My Father in heaven opened your innermost heart to grasp it. And it's on the foundation of that great heart that I will build my church. And not even death will overcome it. I'll give you the keys. Whatever you seal on earth shall be sealed in heaven, and whatever you set free on earth will have that freedom in heaven."

—Matthew 16:13–19

CLOSING

Great Friend,
careful calculation
can take me
only so far.
Amen.

Crucifixion

Quiet my mind. Open my heart. Quicken my soul.

PRESENCE

> Great Friend,
> You suffered so grievously—yet silently—
> to show us how it's done:
> with dignity.
> Amen.

GRACE

> Father, help me see you within the wounded
> along my way.

PSALM

> Who could have thought he'd look like that,
> the power of God like a raggedy scarecrow?
> There was surely nothing appealing in him—
> scorned, spat on, despised, rejected.
> A sack of pain no one wanted to see.
> But . . . but he had volunteered to take our
> place!
> He took our self-crippling into his own flesh.
> He fended off our insults to God
> by offering his pain as a love-gift in our place.

He took the punishment that makes us whole.
In his bruises our deformities heal.
                                    —ISAIAH 53:1–6

HYMN

Friendless and faint, with martyred steps and
    slow,
Faint for the flesh, but for the spirit free,
Stung by the mob that came to see the show,
The Master toiled along to Calvary;
We gibed him, as he went, with houndish
    glee,
Till his dimmed eyes for us did overflow;
We cursed his vengeless hands thrice wretch-
    edly—
And this was nineteen hundred years ago.

But after nineteen hundred years the shame
Still clings, and we have not made good the
    loss
That outraged faith has entered in his name.
Ah, when shall come love's courage to be
    strong!
Tell me, O Lord—tell me, O Lord, how long
Are we to keep Christ writhing on the cross!
                        —EDWIN ARLINGTON ROBINSON

READING

*[Father Barry speaks over the tarpaulin-covered body of
Runty Nolan, murdered by the mob for defying their control
of dockworkers' jobs.]*
  "Some people think the Crucifixion only took place on
Calvary. . . . [But] every time the mob puts the crusher on a
good man, tries to stop him from doing his duty as a union

man and a citizen, it's a crucifixion. And anybody who lets *this* happen"—he gestured toward the tarpaulin—"and I mean *anybody*, from the high and mighty shipping company interests, the Police Commissioner and the DA down to the lowliest worker in the hatch—anybody who keeps silent about something he knows has happened—or strongly suspects has happened—shares the guilt of it just as much as the Roman soldier who pierced the flesh of Our Lord to see if he was dead."

—BUDD SCHULBERG

SCRIPTURE

"Now hear me," Jesus said. "Unless a grain of wheat falls to the ground and dies to itself, it will never be anything else but a trivial grain of wheat. But if it does go through death, then it sprouts new life! Over and over and over again! And in the same way whoever clings to the old ways, fearful of risk and loss, will in fact lose it *all!* But if you're reckless in giving yourself away, how much more alive your life will be, the eternal aliveness of God in the here-and-now!"

—JOHN 12:23–25

CLOSING

Great Friend,
make me love life
more than I fear death.
Amen.

Humility

Quiet my mind. Open my heart. Quicken my soul.

PRESENCE

> Great Friend,
> I will love you
> by making your friends
> feel important.
> Amen.

GRACE

> Father, make me content to warm up your
> audience.

PSALM

> If you hope for mercy, be merciful.
> The clear head must yield to the kind heart.
> Surely, your faith ought to be noticeable.
> What you do gives the laugh to what you
> claim.
> If you run into someone hungry and ragged
> and give them the big "Hel-*lo*, there! How
> ya *doin'*?
> You have a good day, okay?"—
> without even the money for a bowl of soup—
> what right do you have to feel at peace?

47

> Love-talk feeds your ego; love-deeds feed
> their souls.
>
> —JAMES 2:12–17

HYMN

Abide with me; fast falls the eventide;
The darkness deepens; Lord with me abide.
When other helpers fail and comforts flee,
Help of the helpless, Lord, abide with me.

Swift to its close ebbs out life's little day;
Earth's joys grow dim; its glories pass away;
Change and decay in all around I see;
O Thou who changest not, abide with me.

I fear no foe, with Thee at hand to bless;
Ills have no weight, and tears no bitterness.
Where is death's sting? Where, grave, thy
victory?
I triumph still, if Thou abide with me.

—HENRY F. LYTE

READING

Don't imagine that if you meet a really humble man he will be what most people call "humble" nowadays: he won't be a sort of greasy, smarmy person, who's always telling you that, of course, he's nobody. Probably all you'll think about him is that he seemed a cheerful, intelligent chap who took a real interest in what you said to him. If you do dislike him, it will be because you feel a bit envious of anyone who seems to enjoy life so easily. He won't be thinking about himself at all. There I must stop. If anyone would like to acquire humility, I can, I think, tell him the first step. The first step is to realize that one is proud. And a biggish step, too. At least, nothing whatever can be done before it. If you think you're not conceited, it means you are very conceited indeed.

—C. S. Lewis

SCRIPTURE

Jesus rose, took off his outer garments, and tied a towel around his waist. He poured water in a basin and, on his knees he washed their feet one after the other and dried them. But Peter pulled back. "Lord, you can't wash *my* feet."

"Simon," Jesus said, "you don't understand, again. But you will."

Peter was indignantly humble. "You will *never* wash my feet!"

Jesus shook his head and grinned, sadly. "If I don't, we part company."

Peter was completely flustered. "Then wash my hands, Lord, and my head, too!"

"If you've bathed," Jesus said, "that's enough." But he looked around at them.

"You realize what I've done, don't you? If I, the Rabbi, have washed your feet, and you want to be like me, then wash one another's feet—no matter how hesitant each of you might be about it. Do you understand? Even a *bit*? I surely hope so."

—John 13:4–10, 14–15.

CLOSING

> Great Friend,
> make me creatively aware
> of the people
> whose feet
> I would cringe to wash.
> Amen.

Freedom Costs

Quiet my mind. Open my heart. Quicken my soul.

PRESENCE

> Great Friend,
> yielding to your will
> in the way things are made
> will lead me to the self
> you made me to become.
> Amen.

GRACE

> Father, help me understand that freedom
> isn't free.

PSALM

> We're living now in the freedom of God!
> Does that mean we can do anything we
> choose?
> Yes, but our choosing doesn't make it right.
> If we choose to be slaves to attractive un-
> truth,
> we've surrendered free choice to a tyrant.
> God wrote directions for the right use of all
> things

right into the way each is made.
Using them wrongly dishonors them and us.
Using them truly is the freedom of God.

—ROMANS 6:14–18

HYMN

No magic word
can make a wish come true
or weave a web for you
to catch a star.
No magic word
can hold the days of spring
or change the shape of things
from what they are.
How my heart longs to hold
some golden key.
But there is none I know,
and so it's left to me.
No magic word every known
could turn seeds into trees
or now into then.
And so in the end,
It must be me.

—WILLIAM O'MALLEY

READING

Freedom is not merely the opportunity to do as one pleases; neither is it merely the opportunity to choose between set alternatives. Freedom is, first of all, the chance to formulate the available choices, to argue over them—and then, the opportunity to choose.

—C. WRIGHT MILLS

SCRIPTURE

Jesus confronted those who claimed to believe in him. "If you accept what I offer you as the way to live, you will truly be my disciples. You will grasp the truth, and the truth will make you genuinely free."

The worthy gentlemen became a bit huffy at that. "Sir," they said, "you seem to forget we're sons of Abraham. We've never been slaves to anything. What slavery are you claiming your, uh, insights will free us from?"

Jesus answered, "Believe me, anyone who slowly sells out to sin, ever so gradually becomes a slave of sin. But a slave has no firm place in a household, unlike the Son who has the right to do as he pleases—within the pleasure of his Father. If you really were God's own, you wouldn't be secretly plotting against his Son, would you? I'm offering freedom of the household, bequeathed not from earthly parentage, but eternal freedom bestowed from my Father himself."

—John 8:31–38

CLOSING

Great Friend,
keep reminding me:
No one gets freedom
for free.
Amen.

Miracles

Quiet my mind. Open my heart. Quicken my soul.

PRESENCE

>Great Friend,
>so many everyday wonders
>I've taken for granted!
>Wake me up, please.
>Amen.

GRACE

>Father, make me understand how spoiled
>I've been.

PSALM

>Every day of your life rejoice that God loves
>you!
>Luxuriate in it! Let God's kindness shine
>through you!
>Don't brood about anything. Turn worries
>into pleas,
>and God's peace, which outreaches imagina-
>tion,
>will meld your hearts and minds into a
>wholeness,

and Christ will displace disquiet from your
    lives.
Finally, friends, fill your inner selves
with everything that is true, that is noble, just,
genuine, generous, graceful, and gracious.
Focus on what is fine instead of fretting,
and you will find God, shining from all that
    is!

—PHILIPPIANS 4:4–9

HYMN

These I have loved:
White plates and cups, clean-gleaming,
Ringed with blue lines; and feathery, fairy
    dust;
Wet roofs, beneath the lamp-light; the strong
    crust
Of friendly bread; and many-tasting food;
Rainbows; and the blue bitter smoke of
    wood;
And radiant raindrops couching in cool flow-
    ers;
And flowers themselves, that sway through
    sunny hours,
Dreaming of moths that drink them under
    the moon;
Then, the cool kindliness of sheets, that soon
Smooth away trouble; and the rough male
    kiss
Of blankets; grainy wood; live hair that is
Shining and free; blue-massing clouds; the
    keen
Unpassioned beauty of a great machine;
The benison of hot water; furs to touch;

The good smell of old clothes; and other
     such—
The comfortable smell of friendly fingers,
Hair's fragrance, and the musty reek that
     lingers
About dead leaves and last year's ferns.

—RUPERT BROOKE

READING

The test of all happiness is gratitude; and I felt grateful,
though I hardly knew to whom. Children are grateful when
Santa Claus puts in their stockings gifts of toys or sweets.
Could I not be grateful to Santa Claus when he put in my
stockings the gift of two miraculous legs? We thank people
for birthday presents of cigars and slippers. Can I thank no
one for the birthday present of birth?

—G. K. CHESTERTON

SCRIPTURE

Jesus and his disciples came to the synagogue in Nazareth,
his hometown, and many townsfolk gathered to listen to him.
But they were puzzled, turning this way and that, muttering,
"What *is* this?" "I was at *shul* with him. Where does he get
off preaching to us?" "What's going on here?" "They say he
works miracles. That's not true, is it?" "He's the carpenter,
Mary's son. His family are our neighbors. A miracle-worker?
Be serious!"

Jesus shook his head, sadly. "A prophet can't get a hearing,"
he said, "from people who think they know all about him."

They had tied his hands with their refusal to believe. He
healed a few people, but in the end he had to move on. Skep-
tics will never witness miracles.

—MARK 6:1–5

CLOSING

Great Friend,
there is so much more life to life
than I let myself imagine.
Open me to that vitality.
Amen.

Openness

Quiet my mind. Open my heart. Quicken my soul.

PRESENCE

> Great Friend,
> I want to open myself
> to a reality
> far larger, far richer, far more long-lasting
> than the limits of my skin.
> Amen

GRACE

> Father, help me to a deeper hunger for life.

PSALM 139

> Lord, you penetrate every corner of my life.
> You're the life within my every moment.
> Before I speak, you've heard my words.
> Where could I go where you are not?
> If I could fly beyond the farthest star,
> or skimmed the deepest troughs of the sea,
> You would precede and await and greet me
>   there.
> Where you are, there can be neither darkness
>   nor death.

HYMN

The sea awoke at midnight from its sleep,
And round the pebbly beaches far and wide
I heard the first wave of the rising tide
Rush onward with uninterrupted sweep;
A voice out of the silence of the deep,
A sound mysteriously multiplied
As of a cataract from the mountain's side,
Or roar of winds upon a wooded steep.
So comes to us at times, from the unknown
And inaccessible solitudes of being,
The rushing of the sea-tides of the soul;
And inspirations, that we deem our own,
Are some divine foreshadowing and foresee-
      ing
Of things beyond our reason or control.

—HENRY WADSWORTH LONGFELLOW

READING

A human being is a part of the whole called by us "universe," a part limited in time and space. He experiences himself, his thoughts and feeling as something separated from the
rest, a kind of optical delusion of his consciousness. This delusion is a kind of prison for us, restricting us to our personal
desires and to affection for a few persons nearest to us. Our
task must be to free ourselves from this prison by widening
our circle of compassion to embrace all living creatures and
the whole of nature in its beauty.

—ALBERT EINSTEIN

SCRIPTURE

As they pushed through the crowd at the gates of Jericho,
a blind beggar named Bartimaeus sat by the side of the road.
When he heard it was Jesus of Nazareth passing by, he began

to shout, "Jesus! Son of David! Mercy? Please, mercy?" The onlookers tried to hush him up, but he shouted all the louder, "Son of David? Please?"

Jesus turned and said, "Bring him over."

So they said to the blind man, "It worked! Get up! he wants to see you." He threw off his cloak and stumbled toward the voice.

Jesus took his hand and asked, "What do you want me to do for you?"

"Rabbi," the man said, "I want to see."

Jesus massaged the man's thin shoulder. "Done, " he said. "On your way, then. Your faith has healed you and opened your eyes."

Instantly, the man regained his sight and followed Jesus out the gate.

—MARK 10:46–52

CLOSING

Great Friend,
I know
"there are more things in heaven and on
earth
than are dreamt of
in our philosophy"—
or our theology or our physics.
And you stretch far beyond them all.
Amen.

Heart to Heart

Quiet my mind. Open my heart. Quicken my soul.

PRESENCE

> Great Friend,
> let me judge others
> not only with honesty and clarity,
> but also with the same mercy
> I hope for myself.
> Amen.

GRACE

> Father, free me from the need to control.

PSALM

> Dress yourselves so we *see* you are Christ's!
> Wear compassion and kindness. Be humble,
>   patient,
> gentle, tolerant and forgiving of weakness,
> not just in others but in yourself.
> And no matter what else you choose to wear,
> wear love, which binds all else into One.
> Let all your decisions lead to peace
> and all your acts be gifts of thanks.
> —Colossians 3:12–15

HYMN

Make me a pathway of your peace:
Where there is hatred, let me ignite your love;
Where there is hurt, your healing hope,
And where there's doubt, true trust in you.

Make me a pathway of your peace:
Where there are heavy hearts, may I bring
    joy;
Where there is darkness, only light,
And where there's sadness, tireless joy.

O Spirit, help me not to ask
So much to be consoled as to console,
To be understood as to understand,
To be loved as to love with all my soul.

Make me a pathway of your peace.
In mercy, we ourselves are freed,
In sharing all that we ourselves received,
And in dying that we find eternal life.

—SAINT FRANCIS OF ASSISI

READING

When we honestly ask ourselves which person in our lives means the most to us, we often find that it is those who, instead of giving much advice, solutions, or cures, have chosen rather to share our pain and touch our wounds with a gentle and tender hand. The friend who can be silent with us in a moment of despair or confusion, who can stay with us in an hour of grief and bereavement, who can tolerate not knowing, not curing, not healing and face with us the reality of our powerlessness, that is a friend who cares.

—HENRI J. M. NOUWEN

SCRIPTURE

"Once upon a time, a man traveling from Jerusalem to Jericho was jumped by outlaws, beaten, stripped, robbed of all he had, and left half-dead in a ditch. By chance, a priest passed by on the same road, saw the man but quickly diverted his attention and hurried past. Then a Levite, a sort of temple deacon, came by, peered down into the ditch, and tried to think of other things as he went on his way. But a Samaritan, a renegade tribesman Jews instinctively despised, was traveling the same way and saw the beaten man. His heart was filled with pity, so he crawled down to him, did what he could for his wounds, and dragged him up and lifted him onto his own mount. At the next inn he got more help, and the next morning he told the innkeeper to take care of the man and, if there were any further expenses, he'd make good, whatever it cost.

"Which of the three would you say acted like a neighbor?"

—LUKE 10:30–36

CLOSING

Great Friend,
give me the strength
to be yielding.
Amen.

Freedom and Thinking

Quiet my mind. Open my heart. Quicken my soul.

PRESENCE

> Great Friend,
> in order to be truly free
> I have to know
> what all the options are.
> Give me persistence, please.
> (And patience.)
> Amen.

GRACE

> Father, help me make wise choices.

PSALM

> My sisters and brothers, you were called to
>   be free.
> But, like fire, freedom takes a steady hand.
> If you use it badly, it will slip away!
> Be wise and use your freedom, then, to serve,
> because freedom grows in loving hands.
> There you have it, God's entire secret:
> Love. It's what you were created to do.
> It's what raises you above the teeth and talons
> of beasts whose lot is merely to survive.

It's your questing mind that invites you to
    be free!
                                    —GALATIANS 5:13–15

HYMN

Where the mind is without fear and the head
    is held high
Where knowledge is free
Where the world has not been broken up into
    fragments
By narrow domestic walls
Where words come out from the depth of
    truth
Where tireless striving stretches its arms to-
    wards perfection

Where the clear stream of reason has not lost
    its way
Into the dreary desert sand of dead habit
Where the mind is led forward by Thee
Into ever-widening thought and action
Into that heaven of freedom, my Father, let
    my country awake
                            —RABINDRANATH TAGORE

READING

Those who profess to favor freedom and yet depreciate
agitation, are people who want crops without ploughing the
ground; they want rain without thunder and lightning; they
want the ocean without the roar of its many waters. The
struggle may be a moral one, or it may be a physical one,
or it may be both. But it must be a struggle. Power concedes
nothing without a demand; it never has and it never will.
                            —FREDERICK DOUGLASS

SCRIPTURE

Jesus told them, "I'm here to set the whole earth on fire!
And, oh, how I yearn for it to begin to blaze! I've come to
turn all your priorities upside down! I'm here to whirl you
completely around from the way the Beast in you is growl-
ing to go. Do you think I came to bring *security?* And being
unbothered? A living death? I'm not here to simplify your
lives but to complicate them. I'm here to make you stand up
and be *counted.* Even if it means bruised feelings with your
own families. Even if it means they throw you out! The peace
I bring will be within your hearts, my friends, in the way you
face down the world's values."

—LUKE 12:49–53

CLOSING

Great Friend,
you offer us all things
at the price of effort.
I want to accept that.
Amen.

Nearby Saints

Quiet my mind. Open my heart. Quicken my soul.

PRESENCE

> Great Friend,
> make me grateful
> for all those selfless folks
> who passed all kinds of aliveness
> on to me.
> Amen.

GRACE

> Father, let imitation of their kindness be my
> thanks to them.

PSALM

> Do everything openheartedly.
> Go into the world like a breath of life
> among people fixated on merely surviving.
> Let your fire light up their muggy darkness,
> your joy shame the dullness for which they've
> settled.
> You will be proof my teaching was not wasted,
> that the spark of eternal life will pass on
> from heart to heart to the end of time.
> —PHILIPPIANS 2:15–16

66

HYMN

> True Love is founded in rocks of Remem-
>   brance
> In stones of Forbearance and mortar of pain.
> The workman lays wearily granite on granite,
> And bleeds for his castle, 'mid sunshine and
>   rain.
>
> Love is not velvet, not all of it velvet,
> Not all of it banners, not gold-leaf alone.
> 'Tis stern as the ages and old as Religion.
> With Patience its watchword and Law for
>   its throne.

—Vachel Lindsay

READING

On All Saints' Day, it is not just the saints of the church that we should remember in our prayers, but all the foolish ones and wise ones, the shy ones and overbearing ones, the broken ones and whole ones, the despots and tosspots and crackpots of our lives who, one way or another, have been our particular fathers and mothers and saints, and whom we loved without knowing we loved them and by whom we were helped to whatever little we may have, or ever hope to have, of some kind of seedy sainthood of our own.

—Frederick Buechner

SCRIPTURE

"I am the good shepherd, willing to give up everything for my sheep. I'm no hired hand whose heart isn't in his job, who'll run at the first sign of danger and leave the sheep for the wolves. Just as I know my Father and my Father knows me, I know my own and they know me. They know I'm willing to *die* for them."

—John 10:11–15

CLOSING

Great Friend,
help me remember
one by one,
the people to whom I owe
so much.
Amen.

Arrogance

Quiet my mind. Open my heart. Quicken my soul.

PRESENCE

> Great Friend,
> at the core of human evil
> is belief
> that your job
> is still up for grabs.
> Amen.

GRACE

> Father, remind me I've achieved nothing all
> alone.

PSALM 53

> Fools tell themselves, "There is no God!"
> They suck the life from all they touch,
> manhandling it as if they'd taken my place.
> Can there be any hope of honest wisdom,
> in anyone who's failed at trying to be God?
> Can so many be so self-deceived so long?
> They trample the innocent and poison the
> land,
> as if creation won't rise and take revenge.

The scorpion's poisoned lance is poised to
   lunge.
Their blindness to me will become forever
   night.

HYMN

I met a traveller from an antique land
Who said: "Two vast and trunkless legs of
   stone
Stand in the desert. Near them on the sand,
Half sunk, a shattered visage lies, whose
   frown
And wrinkled lip and sneer of cold command
Tell that its sculptor well those passions read
Which yet survive, stamped on these lifeless
   things,
The hand that mocked them and the heart
   that fed.
And on the pedestal these words appear:
`My name is Ozymandias, King of Kings:
Look on my works, ye mighty, and despair!'
Nothing beside remains. Round the decay
Of that colossal wreck, boundless and bare,
The lone and level sands stretch far away.

—Percy Bysshe Shelley

READING

"I got this today," they say; "tomorrow I shall get that. This
wealth is mine, and that will be mine too. I have destroyed my
enemies. I shall destroy others too! Am I not like God? I enjoy
what I want. I am undefeated. Potent! Carefree! I am rich and
well-born. Who is my equal? I will perform rituals and give
alms, and rejoice in my own unselfishness." This is how they

jabber, unbalanced as they are. Bound by greed and webbed in illusion, whirled into fragmented minds, they stumble into hell. Preening, stubborn, tumbled about by the arrogance of wealth, they pretentiously perform sacrifices within their lead cocoons. Conceited, hostile, cocksure, lewd, raging, envious of everyone, they abuse my presence within their own bodies and in the bodies of others."

—BHAGAVAD GITA

SCRIPTURE

Jesus told this to people who found the best way to look at others was down the length of their noses. "Two men went into the Temple. One was a Pharisee who'd established his piety with great care; the other was a tax collector whose well-cut clothes could never disguise his crooked reputation. The Pharisee assumed a pose and said, almost aloud, 'Ah, God! I'm *so* grateful I'm not like so many others—thieves, scoundrels, adulterers, or like that sticky-fingered collaborator back there. I fast twice a week. I give a tenth of my income. I hope you're as pleased with me as I am.' But the tax man huddled in the back, hiding his face, 'God, have mercy on me. I'm such a contemptible sinner.'"

"I tell you, that tax collector went home in God's love. But the self-righteous one? If you can justify yourself, then you don't need God, do you? You can fall on your face all by yourself."

—LUKE 18:9–14

CLOSING

> Great Friend,
> help me walk the razor wire
> between honest confidence
> and self-delusion.
> Amen.

One Aliveness

Quiet my mind. Open my heart. Quicken my soul.

PRESENCE

> Great Friend,
> you are the pool of existence
> out of which everything draws its "is"—
> You are the Energy
> that whirls the tiny molecule
> and the measureless galaxy,
> and me.
> Amen.

GRACE

> Father, let me somehow feel your divine life
> within everything.

PSALM

> Christ is the bodying forth of the invisible
> God.
> He is God's original idea of all that is.
> Through him, everything that is—*every-*
> *thing*—
> in heaven and on earth, seen and unseen,
> beyond the human power to imagine, *all*
> originated in him and finds its purpose there.

And now he is the head of his body, the
    church,
and his Spirit is the well of its life.
He is the firstborn from the dead, to lead us
    home.
In him, everything fits together once again!

                —COLOSSIANS 1:15–20

HYMN

O world, I cannot hold thee close enough!
Thy winds, thy wide grey skies!
Thy mists, that roll and rise!
Thy woods, this autumn day, that ache and
    sag
And all but cry with colour! That gaunt crag
To crush! To lift the lean of that black bluff!
World, world, I cannot get thee close enough!

Long have I known a glory in it all,
But never knew I this;
Here such a passion is
As stretcheth me apart, —Lord, I do fear
Thou'st made the world too beautiful this
    year;
My soul is all but out of me, —let fall
No burning leaf; prithee, let no bird call.

             —EDNA ST. VINCENT MILLAY

READING

The same stream of life that runs through my veins night
and day runs through the world and dances in rhythmic
measures. It is the same life that shoots in joy through the
dust of the earth in numberless blades of grass and breaks
into tumultuous waves of leaves and flowers. It is the same
life that is rocked in the ocean-cradle of birth and of death,

in ebb and in flow. I feel my limbs are made glorious by the touch of this world of life. And my pride is from the life-throb of ages dancing in my blood this moment.

—RABINDRANATH TAGORE

SCRIPTURE

In the beginning was the Word—God's self-expression— who was with God and one with God. Through him, God made all that exists. Not one thing ever came into being that didn't find its way through him. The Word was the source of all life, and that life is the light of all humankind. That light shines in the darkness, and no conceivable darkness could quench that light.

—JOHN 1:1–5

CLOSING

Great Friend,
There's a spark of you—
gasp!—
in *me!*
Help me be unashamed to make it
shine!
Amen.

Unworthiness

Quiet my mind. Open my heart. Quicken my soul.

PRESENCE

>Great Friend,
>when people I trust agree
>that it is probably you who call me,
>grant me to grasp
>that you know my limits
>better than I do.
>Amen.

GRACE

>Father, only my refusal can block what you
>can do with me.

PSALM

>In the year King Uzziah died, I saw the Lord.
>He sat enthroned among creatures with fiery
>wings,
>chanting, "Holy, holy, holy is the Lord of
>Hosts!
>The whole universe trembles with his glory!"
>"Oh, God!" I groaned. "I'm surely doomed!
>My mouth befouls all that I speak.

And yet my unworthy eyes have beheld the
  Lord!"
Then one of the fiery beings flew to me,
carrying a blistering coal from the altar.
The creature touched my mouth with it and
  said,
"See! This living coal has touched your lips
and burned away your unworthiness!"
Then I heard the voice of the Lord thunder:
"Whom shall I send? Who will go for us?"
And I heard a tiny voice cry, "Here!
Here I am. Send me."
And I realized the voice was mine.

—Isaiah 6:1–8

HYMN

Love bade me welcome, yet my soul drew
  back,
Guilty of dust and sin.
But quick-eyed Love, observing me grow
  slack
From my first entrance in,
Drew nearer to me, sweetly questioning
If I lacked anything.

"A guest," I answered, "worthy to be here";
Love said, "You shall be he."
"I, the unkind, the ungrateful? ah my dear,
I cannot look on Thee."
Love took my hand and smiling did reply,
"Who made the eyes but I?"

"Truth, Lord, but I have marred them; let
  my shame
Go where it doth deserve."

"And know you not," says Love, "who bore
     the blame?"
"My dear, then I will serve."
"You must sit down," says Love, "and taste
     my meat."
So I did sit and eat.

—George Herbert

READING

I decline to accept the end of man. It is easy enough to say that man is immortal simply because he will endure: that when the last ding-dong of doom has clanged and faded from the last worthless rock hanging tideless in the last red and dying evening, that even then there will still be one more sound: that of his puny inexhaustible voice, still talking. I refuse to accept this. I believe that man will not merely endure: he will prevail. He is immortal, not because he alone among creatures has an inexhaustible voice, but because he has a soul, a spirit capable of compassion and sacrifice and endurance.

—William Faulkner

SCRIPTURE

They came to the place called Gethsemane, and Jesus said to his friends, "Sit here while I pray." he took the stalwarts with him—Peter, James, and John—and moved off a bit into the trees. Suddenly, he sank into himself, like a man sucked into a swamp of anguish. He could hardly get his breath as he said to them, "The terror in my heart is so fierce it's devouring me. Stay with me! Please?"

He went a little further alone and collapsed again to his knees, clutching his arms around his belly, rocking in torment. He begged God with all the power within him—to change his mind, to find some other way. "Father!" he groaned. "O God, my Father, listen to me! All things are possible to you, but not

to *me!* Take this cup of suffering away from me. *Please!* But
. . . but not what I think I can do. Not what I want. Let it be
what you want me to try."

—MARK 14:32–36

CLOSING

> Great Friend,
> into your hands
> I commend my spirit—
> and everything else I have.
> Amen.

The Really Real

Quiet my mind. Open my heart. Quicken my soul.

PRESENCE

> Great Friend,
> remind me—often—
> that only you
> see clearly the inner truth
> of all that is.
> Amen.

GRACE

> Father, make me humble about my first impressions. And my second.

PSALM

> Our message is hidden only from the self-
>   blinded,
> who choose what they will or will not allow
>   to be real,
> who succumb to the promise that darkness
>   is light.
> The world's god blinds them from the truth,
> from seeing God's light shining from within
>   themselves.
> God gives this vision to see inner truth

to those who don't put themselves in Truth's
way.

—2 Corinthians 4:3–9

HYMN

A young spring-tender girl
combed her joyous hair
'You are very ugly' said the mirror.
But, on her lips hung
a smile of dove-secret loveliness,
for only that morning had not
the blind boy said,
'You are beautiful'?

—Spike Milligan[3]

READING

The little prince went back to the fox.
"Goodbye," he said.
"Goodbye," said the fox. "Now here is my secret, a very
simple secret: It is only with the heart that one can see rightly;
what is essential is invisible to the eye."
"What is essential is invisible to the eye," the little prince
repeated, so that he would be sure to remember.

—Antoine de St. Exupery

SCRIPTURE

Once when Jesus was walking through Jericho, there was
a squat little man named Zacchaeus, a rich but detestable
tax collector, who really wanted to get a look at this teacher
everybody was talking about. But he was too short to see over
the heads of his neighbors, who weren't about to let the little
crook squeeze in front. So Zacchaeus trotted along behind the

---

[3] Spike Milligan, "Mirror, Mirror." Used with permission.

onlookers till he came to a sycamore tree and shinnied up it to get a better view.

When Jesus came along and looked up at this fat monkey of a man peering down at him, he suppressed a giggle and said, "Zacchaeus, come down from there! I want to spend the day with you!"

Dumbfounded, the little fellow scurried down and almost tripped over himself with joy, leading a *preacher* into *his* house! The neighbors were livid, not knowing whether to sneer more at Zacchaeus or at Jesus for even speaking to the detestable runt.

At lunch, Zacchaeus fumbled to his feet and stammered, "Sir, I will give half what I own to the poor. And if I have cheated anyone, I swear I will pay back four times as much."

Jesus looked at him with a quiet grin. "My friend," he said, "salvation has entered your home today. I have come for just such as you, the seemingly lost."

—LUKE 19: 1–10

CLOSING

> Great Friend,
> I also need reminding
> that anything repellent,
> once it's loved,
> becomes beautiful.
> Amen.

Working

Quiet my mind. Open my heart. Quicken my soul.

PRESENCE

> Great Friend,
> make me value
> not being paid by the hour
> but from what I bring to the hour.
> Amen.

GRACE

> Father, allow me to be justifiably proud at the
> end of the day.

PSALM

> Workers, regard your supervisors with respect
> as if you were serving the requests of Christ.
> Your true self is the person you are
> when no one's watching or judging you.
> You need no one's approval but the Lord's,
> and he reads only the intentions of your
> heart.
> Remember: whether you obey or give orders,
> what the Lord rewards is your sincere striv-
> ing.

—EPHESIANS 6:5–8

HYMN

Work is love made visible.
And if you cannot work with love
But only with distaste,
It is better
That you should leave your work
And sit at the gate of the temple
And take alms from those
Who work with joy.

—AUTHOR UNKNOWN

READING

What work I have done I have done because it has been play. If it had been work I shouldn't have done it. Who was it who said, "Blessed is the man who has found his work"? Whoever it was, he had the right idea in his mind. Mark you, he says his work—not somebody else's work. The work that is really a man's own work is play and not work at all. Cursed is the man who has found some other man's work and cannot lose it. When we talk about the great workers of the world we really mean the great players of the world. The fellows who groan and sweat under the weary load of toil that they bear never can hope to do anything great. How can they when their souls are in a ferment of revolt against the employment of their hands and brains? The product of slavery, intellectual or physical, can never be great.

—MARK TWAIN

SCRIPTURE

Paul began to say his farewells to the elders of the Christian community in Ephesus. "I leave you now in the hands of God and his grace, the inheritance of those sanctified in Christ. You all know that when I worked among you, I never envied anyone else's money or clothing but worked with these very hands to support myself and my companions. I trust you'll follow that example, in the conviction that by hard work we have to support not only ourselves but the weak who cannot help themselves. As the Lord said, 'You're more enviable when you're giving than when you're getting.'"

—ACTS 20:32–35

CLOSING

> Great Friend,
> help me find
> a way to serve
> with passion and joy.
> Amen.

Excuses

Quiet my mind. Open my heart. Quicken my soul.

PRESENCE

> Great Friend,
> I want to learn that
> alibis and procrastination
> and lack of foresight and denial
> and scapegoating are—
> none of them—
> incurable diseases.
> Amen.

GRACE

> Father, help me understand that silence means
> consent.

PSALM

> Way, way back, when snakes still spoke
> and fast-talked the woman into outsmarting
>   God,
> she ate some of the forbidden fruit
> and felt so high and filled with insights,
> she gave some to her husband, and it thrilled
>   him, too.
> But one of the never-before insights they got

was that they, well, had no clothes on.
So they patched some together from leaves.
That evening as God was strolling in the
    Garden,
they hid from him in shame, till God called.
They sidled out and stammered, "We hid
because we were, uh, ashamed . . . to be . . .
    uh . . . naked."
God took a deep breath, "So," he sighed,
"you've discovered 'naked.' You ate from the
    tree."
"The *woman*!" the man said, "that woman
you put me with! She *made* me do it!"
And God asked the woman, "Why?"
She said, "The *snake*! The snake *tricked* me
    into it!"

          —GENESIS 3:6–13

HYMN

In Germany, they came first for the Com-
    munists,
and I didn't speak,
because I wasn't a Communist.
Then they came for the Jews,
and I didn't speak,
because I wasn't a Jew.
Then they came for the trade unionists,
and I didn't speak,
because I wasn't a trade unionist.
Then they came for the Catholics,
and I didn't speak,
because I was a Protestant.
Then they came for me,
and by that time,
no one was left to stand up.

          —PASTOR MARTIN NEIMOELLER

READING

Now is the accepted time, not tomorrow, not some more convenient season.

It is today that our best work can be done and not some future day or future year.

It is today that we fit ourselves for the greater usefulness of tomorrow. Today is the seed time, now are the hours of work, and tomorrow comes the harvest and the playtime

—W. E. B. Du Bois

SCRIPTURE

"If you want to understand the kingdom, think of once-upon-a-time. Once there were ten young bridesmaids waiting to escort the bridegroom and his party to the house of the bride's father. Five of them were silly and had brought lamps but no oil, and five were prudent and brought both. But the bridegroom was delayed and delayed, so all the girls began to droop and doze, while the flames of their lamps danced for a while and then flickered out.

"Suddenly, with no real warning, they were jolted awake by the groomsmen shouting, 'Here we come, ladies!' They scurried around, trying to get their lamps going again. The shortsighted ones tried to talk the wise ones into sharing their oil. But the clever girls scowled and snapped, 'Then *all* the lamps will go out before we get there!'

"So off the silly ones went, trying to scare up oil with all the shops closed. When they finally got to the wedding feast and hammered on the doors, the banquet was in full swing. They asked to be let in, but from within came a voice that shouted, 'Go away! Nobody knows you here.'"

And Jesus ended, "How will you know you waited too long?"

—Matthew 25:1–13

CLOSING

> Great Friend,
> I take full responsibility
> for everything I do—
> or don't.
> Amen.

Useful = Used

Quiet my mind. Open my heart. Quicken my soul.

PRESENCE

> Great Friend,
> the cautious voices in me counsel
> "Keep your guard up,"
> "Watch your back,"
> "They're *using* you!"
> Let me challenge those demons
> with a crucifix.
> Amen.

GRACE

> Father, help me invest myself fully in the life
> you've given me.

PSALM

> A pinch-penny planter gets a stingy crop.
> An extravagant planter gets a lavish crop.
> When you decide what you'll give, you decide
> what you'll get.
> Give neither with regret nor from grim sense
> of duty.
> Give because that's what you were *born* to
> do!

When you're generous, God will outdo you
so you'll always have enough and to spare.
Scripture describes those who understand:
"They give incautiously, with both hands.
There is no limit to their kindness."

—2 CORINTHIANS 9:6–9

HYMN

Take and receive, O Lord, my liberty.
Take all my will, my mind, and memory.
All things I have, and all I own are thine.
Thine was the gift, to thee, I all resign.

Do thou direct and govern all and sway,
Do what thou wilt: Command, and I obey.
Only thy grace and love on me bestow.
Possessing these, all else I will forego.

—IGNATIUS LOYOLA

READING

This is the true joy in life, the being used for a purpose
recognized by yourself as a mighty one; the being thoroughly
worn out before you are thrown on the scrap heap; the being a force of nature instead of a feverish selfish little clod of
ailments and grievances complaining that the world will not
devote itself to making you happy.

—GEORGE BERNARD SHAW

SCRIPTURE

When the other disciples heard that James and John (and
their pushy mother) had been finagling with Jesus about
having influential places, they blew up. So Jesus called them
together to try, yet again, to straighten out their priorities.
"You know that, in the world, power is oh-so-precious to

those of small minds. They get their self-esteem by pushing others around, by kidding themselves they have more power than they do. It's *not* going to be that way with us. Do you understand me? If you really want to be great, then you've got to serve all the others. You become valuable when people take advantage of your value. Isn't that what I've done? Isn't it clear yet that I've come to serve, not to be served? Even with my life."

—MARK 10:41–45

CLOSING

> Great Friend,
> maturity comes
> when we prefer
> the active to the passive.
> Amen.

Feeling Lost

Quiet my mind. Open my heart. Quicken my soul.

PRESENCE

> Great Friend,
> they say Saint Teresa told you,
> "If you treat all your friends,
> the way you've been treating me,
> I'm not surprised you have so few."
> A most insightful woman.
> Not to mention gutsy.
> Amen.

GRACE

> Father, take my hand in the dark.

PSALM

> When Jesus said, "You must eat my flesh
> and drink my blood for undying life,"
> a number quietly drifted away.
> So he said to the rest, "Will you go, too?
> When what I say defies belief,
> will the fact *I* say it be enough?
> No one can accept it without God's help."
> He looked around from face to face:
> "And you," he asked, "will you leave now?"
> Simon Peter huffed, "Lord,

where else in the world would I go?
We hardly understand a word you say,
but we *know* what you say is the truth."

—JOHN 6:60–69

HYMN

Your hope in my heart is the rarest treasure
Your Name on my tongue the sweetest word
My choicest hours
Are the hours I spend with You—
O Allah, I can't live in this world
Without remembering You—
How can I endure the next world
Without seeing Your face?
I am a stranger in Your country
And lonely among Your worshipers:
This is the substance of my complaint.

—RABIA AL BASRI

READING

The soul has to go on loving in the emptiness, or at least to go on *wanting* to love, though it may only be with an infinitesimal part of itself. Then, one day, God will come to show himself to this soul and to reveal the beauty of the world to it, as in the case of Job. But if the soul stops loving, it falls—even in this life—into something almost equivalent to hell.

—SIMONE WEIL

SCRIPTURE

At noon, darkness spread over the whole countryside, and about three o'clock, Jesus raised his battered head a bit and gasped, "Eli, Eli, lema sabachtani?" which means, "My God, my God, why have you abandoned me?"

—MATTHEW 27:45–46

CLOSING

Great Friend,
I do believe.
Help my unbelief.
Amen.

Zombie "Love"

Quiet my mind. Open my heart. Quicken my soul.

PRESENCE

> Great Friend,
> I honestly want to be
> who I like to tell myself
> I am.
> Amen.

GRACE

> Father, help me love with a truly open
>   heart.

PSALM

> Pretense and lip-service are not enough.
> What you *do* outshouts whatever you claim.
> Half-hearing is like taking a look at yourself,
> just long enough to forget who you *are*.
> But see yourself in the mirror of Christ
> who frees you from all pretenses and posing.
> The genuine joy your giving gives
> proves what you call religion is truth.
>
> —JAMES 1:22–25

HYMN

> My enemy came nigh,
> And I
> Stared fiercely in his face.
> My lips went writhing back in a grimace,
> And stern I watched him with a narrow eye.
> Then, as I turned away, my enemy,
> That bitter heart and savage, said to me:
> "Some day, when this is past,
> When all the arrows that we have are cast,
> We may ask one another why we hate,
> And fail to find a story to relate.
> It may seem then to us a mystery
> That we should hate each other."
> Thus said he,
> And did not turn away,
> Waiting to hear what I might have to say.
> But I fled quickly, fearing had I stayed
> I might have kissed him as I would a maid.
>
> —James Stephens

READING

The word *sin* is somehow too grand a word to apply to the reaction of the prodigal's elder brother when the sound of the hoedown reaches him out in the pasture among the cow flops, yet in another way it is just the right word because nowhere is the deadliness of all seven deadly sins deadlier or more ludicrous than it is in him. Envy and pride and anger and covetousness are all there. Even sloth is there as he sits on his patrimony and lets it gain interest for him without lifting a hand, even lust as he slavers over the harlots whom he points out the prodigal has squandered his cash on. The elder brother is Pecksniff. He is Tartuffe. He is what Mark Twain called a good man in the worst sense of the word.

—Frederick Buechner

SCRIPTURE

"God help you moralists and Pharisees! You give the Temple 10 percent of your garden herbs and weeds and completely ignore the guts of the Law—fairness, compassion, honesty! Being finicky misses the whole *point*! Blind guides! You pinch a fly from your soup and gulp down a camel!

"God help you moralists and Pharisees! Hypocrites! You wash the outsides of your bowls and cups and leave the insides clotted with greed and pettiness. Clean up your hearts, and let them shine through the surfaces.

"God help you moralists and Pharisees! Frauds! You're like whitewashed tombs, dazzling on the outside and maggoty and decayed inside. You're experts at posing, but inside you're empty men!"

—Matthew 23:23–28

CLOSING

Great Friend,
it's wrong, I know,
to fool anyone,
but worst of all
myself.
Amen.

God/Man

Quiet my mind. Open my heart. Quicken my soul.

PRESENCE

> Great Friend,
> my belief that you
> infused divinity into humanity
> ought to impel me
> to expect more of myself.
> Amen.

GRACE

> Father, help me accept an ennobling I did
>   nothing to deserve.

PSALM

> He was never anything else but God,
> but he didn't cling to the powers that reside
>   in God.
> Instead, he gave it all up—*emptied* himself—
> in order to become in every way as humans are.
> He lived a selfless, obedient life—and death,
> not just death, but excruciating death on a
>   cross.
> Because of that, God raised him up
> and returned to him the divine name and place.

Thus, all beings—in heaven, on earth, and in
    hell—
should bow in worship before the name of
    Jesus
and every voice confess Jesus Christ is LORD!
                —PHILIPPIANS 2:6–11

HYMN

For unto us a child is born,
unto us a son is given:
and the government shall be upon
his shoulder: and his name
shall be called:
Wonderful, Counsellor,
The mighty God,
The everlasting Father,
The Prince of Peace.
       —GEORG FRIEDRICH HANDEL (ISAIAH 9:6)

READING

People often say about Him: "I'm ready to accept Jesus as a great moral teacher, but I don't accept His claim to be God." That is the one thing we must not say. A man who was merely a man and said the sort of things Jesus said would not be a great moral teacher. He would either be a lunatic—on a level with the man who says he is a poached egg—or else he would be the Devil of Hell. You must make your choice. Either this man was, and is, the Son of God: or else a madman or something worse. You can shut Him up for a fool, you can spit at Him and kill Him as a demon; or you can fall at His feet and call Him Lord and God. But let us not come with any patronizing nonsense about His being a great human teacher. He has not left that open to us. He did not intend to.
       —C. S. LEWIS

SCRIPTURE

Then the people picked up stones to throw at Jesus, but he held up his hand. "I've done good actions among you. Which one do you stone me for?"

They were flabbergasted at his arrogance. "We're not going to stone you for any good deed! You deserve to be stoned for making yourself *God*!"

Jesus chuckled dryly. "Your own scriptures have God saying, 'You are gods, sons of the Most High.' Will you stone the scriptures, too? How can you stone me for a blasphemer when I truly *am* the one my Father chose and sent into the world? One-of-a-kind! If I do anything that conflicts with my Father's will, then condemn me. But if you don't believe what I claim, you ought at least to believe what I do, what you see with your own eyes! Then you might see that the Father is *in* me, and I am *in* the Father!"

—JOHN 10:31–38

CLOSING

Great Friend,
let me leave aside
the unanswerable questions
about *how* you pulled off
fusing divinity and humanity.
You have more important
tasks for me.
Amen.

The Shadow

Quiet my mind. Open my heart. Quicken my soul.

PRESENCE

>   Great Friend,
>   inside myself
>   I find a grab-bag of faults and virtues,
>   many of which are hard to evaluate.
>   Help me make creative use
>   of them all.
>   Amen.

GRACE

>   Father, help me understand I needn't apolo-
>   gize for being human.

PSALM

>   The greatest mystery for me is myself.
>   I make up my mind to do what's right—
>   and then I turn round and do what I hate!
>   Since, by myself, I can't be trusted,
>   it's pretty clear I need some wise guidance
>   from people whom the child in me resents.
>   I've got a weakness deep inside my soul,
>   a selfishness I share with other beasts.
>   But the desire for goodness that I also feel

tells me God doesn't want me to settle for
that.

—ROMANS 7:15–20

HYMN

On a rusty iron throne
Past the furthest star of space
I saw Satan sit alone,
Old and haggard was his face;
For his work was done and he
Rested in eternity.
    And to him from out the sun
    Came his father and his friend
    Saying, now the work is done
    Enmity is at an end:
    And he guided Satan to
    Paradises that he knew.
Gabriel without a frown,
Uriel without a spear,
Raphael came singing down
Welcoming their ancient peer,
And they seated him beside
One who had been crucified

—JAMES STEPHENS (B. 1882)

READING

Simon felt a perilous necessity to speak; but to speak in
assembly was a terrible thing to him.

"Maybe," he said hesitantly, "maybe there *is* a Beast."

The assembly cried out savagely and Ralph stood up in
amazement.

"You, Simon? You believe in this?"

"I don't know," said Simon. His heartbeats were choking
him. "But . . ."

Ralph shouted. "Hear him! He's got the conch!"
"What I mean is . . . maybe it's only us."

—WILLIAM GOLDING

SCRIPTURE

"Once upon a time, a man sowed good seed in his fields. But during the night, while everyone on the farm was asleep, an enemy crept into the fields and sowed weeds among the wheat from one end to the other. Later, when the plants grew and the grains began to form in the husks, the hands saw that the fields were patchy with weeds, so they went to the boss and asked how it could have happened. The farmer realized someone had it in for him, but when the hands asked if they should pull up the weeds, he said, 'No. If we do, we're bound to uproot a lot of good wheat along with them. Let them grow together till harvest. Then we'll be able to do the job right.'"

—MATTHEW 13:25–30

CLOSING

Great Friend,
remind me again of the alchemists
who turned lead into gold.
Amen.

Spunk

Quiet my mind. Open my heart. Quicken my soul.

PRESENCE

> Great Friend,
> in a world that honors
> cunning, superficiality, pretense,
> where commitments hinge
> on convenience,
> empower me to stand firm,
> as my honest self.
> Amen.

GRACE

> Father, once I'm resolved, keep me resilient.

PSALM

> I'd be the last to claim I've got it made.
> It's the striving that counts, not the achieve-
> ment.
> I'm straining forward on the course Christ
> ran,
> heading for the goal where he waits for me.
> No, no! I'm nowhere near a winner yet!
> The past's behind. My eyes are fixed ahead
> on Jesus, who's cheering me all the way.
>
> —Philippians 3:12–14

HYMN

O dandelion, rich and haughty,
King of village flowers!
For you each day is coronation time,
You have no humble hours.
I like to see you bring a troop
To beat the blue-grass spears,
To scorn the lawn-mower that would be
Like fate's triumphant shears,
Your yellow heads are cut away,
It seems your reign is o'er.
By noon you raise a sea of stars
More golden than before.

—Vachel Lindsay

READING

I believe in aristocracy, though—if that is the right word, and if a democrat may use it. Not an aristocracy of power, based upon rank and influence, but an aristocracy of the sensitive, the considerate and the plucky. Its members are to be found in all nations and classes, and all through the ages, and there is a secret understanding between them when they meet. They represent the true human tradition, the one permanent victory of our queer race over cruelty and chaos. Thousands of them perish in obscurity, a few are great names. They are sensitive for others as well as for themselves, they are considerate without being fussy, their pluck is not swankiness but the power to endure, and they can take a joke.

—E. M. Forster

SCRIPTURE

"Once upon a time, there was a hatchet-faced judge as unconcerned about human opinion as he was about God's. But in the same town was a feisty widow who kept coming

to him for a judgment against her creditors. The judge treated
her like a bad smell. But the old lady wouldn't be fobbed off.
She button-holed worthy villagers in the streets, shrieked her
woes at prostitutes under the judge's windows, burdened any
foreigner with her woes in a squawk that echoed for blocks.
Finally, the judge was fit to choke this unbearable hag. 'No
power in heaven or earth could cork this cantankerous crone!
Either I give her her judgment or go stark raving bonkers!'"
So he caved in.

—LUKE 18:1–5

CLOSING

Great Friend,
remind me always
that the most open mind
is an empty head.
Amen.

Friendship

Quiet my mind. Open my heart. Quicken my soul.

PRESENCE

> Great Friend,
> when I'm tempted to self-pity,
> make me remember
> to mull over the faces
> of those I truly love
> in order to see
> I have no excuse for that.
> Amen.

GRACE

> Father, help me never to take those I love for
> granted.

PSALM

> Naomi, a Hebrew widow, lived
> with her pagan Moabite daughters-in-law,
> Orpah and Ruth, who were also widowed.
> When Naomi resolved to return to her
> people,
> the younger women wanted to come,
> but she said they must stay and find husbands
> while she returned home to await her death.

So Orpah turned back, but Ruth refused.
"Don't ask me to leave," the girl said.
"Wherever you go, I will go.
Wherever you live, I will live, too.
Your people will be my people,
and your God will be my God, too."

—RUTH 1:6–16

HYMN

They came to tell your faults to me,
They named them over one by one;
I laughed aloud when they were done,
I knew them all so well before,—
Oh, they were blind, too blind to see
Your faults had made me love you more.

—SARA TEASDALE

READING

Oh, the comfort, the inexpressible comfort of feeling safe with a person; having neither to weigh thoughts nor to measure words but to pour them all out, just as it is, chaff and grain together, knowing that a faithful hand will take and sift them, keeping what is worth keeping, and then, with the breath of kindness, blow the rest away.

—GEORGE ELIOT

SCRIPTURE

[When Jesus and his disciples heard that Lazarus was deathly ill, they made their way slowly to Jerusalem, even though Jesus—and the more cautious of his men, like Thomas—knew coming to Jerusalem was begging to be arrested. On the way, they discovered Lazarus was now three days dead, and both Lazarus's sisters hinted that, if he had wanted, Jesus could have been there earlier to prevent it.] Jesus saw the sisters and their servants weeping, and his heart was shaken as they led him to the burial place.

When they arrived, Jesus stood silent, weeping for his friend. Some said, "See how much he loved him?" But he heard others sneering, "Really? he saved that blind man. Why didn't he save Lazarus if he was such a friend?"

But Jesus, knowing there were even weightier reasons for his coming to Jerusalem this one last time, wept even more. "Take the stone away," he said.

But Martha pushed forward. "No, master. He's been dead four days. There will be a smell."

Jesus said, "Didn't I tell you you'd see God's glory if you believed?" So they moved the stone and, after he prayed, Jesus cried, "Lazarus! Come out!"

And there in the doorway stood the corpse, wrapped head to foot in his grave bindings, with a cloth over his face.

"Unbind him," Jesus said, "and let him go."

—JOHN 11

CLOSING

> Great Friend,
> remind me that
> the test of genuine friendship
> is the willingness to risk intruding.
> Amen.

Resentment

Quiet my mind. Open my heart. Quicken my soul.

PRESENCE

> Great Friend,
> help me
> sever the grudges
> that hold me
> down.
> Amen.

GRACE

> Remind me: Resentment is like taking poison
> and hoping the other guy dies.

PSALM

> Remember the older son who stayed at home.
> He trudged in weary from the stubborn fields
> and heard the whole bunch in happy ca-
> rouse—
> on *his* food and wine. Let's be mindful of
> that.
> When he asked why the ruckus, some kitchen
> kid shot back,
> "Your brother's come home, and your dad
> threw him a party!"

Well, the brother squatted and grumped and
    refused to go in.
His father, suddenly sad, came out to plead.
But filled with bitter righteousness, the boy
    held firm:
"All my life, I've galley-slaved for you!
Day after day, and not so much as 'Thanks!'
But this do-nothing took half your lifetime's
    work,
squandered it on booze and whores, and
    you—
you give him the key to start it all again?"
"But son," his father said, "all that's yours
    was mine,
the other half of my whole lifetime's toil.
From all I gave you, can't you spare one
    feast?
Your brother was dead and came back to us
    alive!"
But the boy preferred to feed on wrath and
    tears.

—LUKE 15:25–32

HYMN

When to the sessions of sweet silent thought
I summon up remembrance of things past,
I sigh the lack of many a thing I sought,
And with old woes new wail my dear time's
    waste:
Then can I drown an eye, unused to flow,
For precious friends hid in death's dateless
    night,
And weep afresh love's long since cancell'd
    woe,
And moan the expense of many a vanish'd
    sight:

Then can I grieve at grievances foregone,
And heavily from woe to woe tell o'er
The sad account of fore-bemoaned moan,
Which I new pay as if not paid before.
But if the while I think on thee, Dear Friend,
All losses are restored and sorrows end.
—WILLIAM SHAKESPEARE

READING

And acceptance is the answer to all my problems today. When I am disturbed, it is because I find some person, place, thing, or situation—some fact of my life—unacceptable to me, and I can find no serenity until I accept that person, place, thing, or situation as being exactly the way it is supposed to be at this moment. Nothing, absolutely nothing happens in God's world by mistake. Until I could accept my alcoholism, I could not stay sober; unless I accept life completely on life's terms, I cannot be happy. I need to concentrate not so much on what needs to be changed in the world as on what needs to be changed in me and in my attitudes.
—*THE BIG A.A. BOOK*

SCRIPTURE

When evening came, the vineyard owner called his foreman. "Call the pickers and pay them their wages. But start with the ones we hired an hour ago, then work back to those we hired first thing this morning." The workers who started at five got a silver coin each. So, obviously, the ones who'd worked the full day just assumed they'd get ten times as much. Their lucky day!

But when they came to the foreman, they got only one silver coin, too—the regular daily wage. They looked at it cupped in their calloused paws and started to grumble and bellyache. "What gives here? We got here *first*, right? And these bums, standin' around all day, get the same as us?

Breakin' our backs and the skin peelin' off us in the sun?
Come *on*!"

The owner came out and said, "Friends, have I cheated any
one of you? This morning we agreed on your wages, yes? I
wanted these last ones hired to be able to feed their kids, too.
Can't I decide what I do with my own money? Or are you
grousing because I'm generous?"

[There is no record of their response.]

—MATTHEW 20: 8–15

CLOSING

> Great Friend,
> after all you've given,
> how could I dare
> begrudge anyone
> having better?
> Amen.

Curiosity

Quiet my mind. Open my heart. Quicken my soul.

PRESENCE

> Great Friend,
> help me to distrust
> what "everybody" says
> and "everybody" knows
> and "everybody" does.
> Amen.

GRACE

> Father, you did not create me to be a witless
>   sheep.

PSALM

> Our faith isn't rooted solely in cold reasoning.
> It takes God's Spirit to melt through to truth.
> They can grasp it who can go *beyond* intellect
> and the world's cramping calculations.
> If they had been able to grasp God's intent,
> would they have executed his Messenger?
> Because no merely human mind could fathom
> what God has readied for those who trust
>   in him.

—1 CORINTHIANS 2:5–9

HYMN

When I heard the learn'd astronomer,
When the proofs, the figures, were ranged in
columns before me,
When I was shown the charts, the diagrams,
to add, divide, and measure them,
When I, sitting, heard the learned astronomer
where he lectured with much applause
in the lecture room,
How soon unaccountable I became tired and
sick,
Till rising and gliding out I wander'd off by
myself,
In the mystical moist night-air, and from time
to time,
Look'd up in perfect silence at the stars.

—WALT WHITMAN

READING

"Don't believe anything simply because you've heard it. Don't believe anything simply because it's spoken and rumored by many. Don't believe in anything simply because it's found written in your religious books. Don't believe in anything merely on the authority of your teachers and elders. Don't believe in traditions because they've been handed down for many generations. But after observation and analysis, when you find that anything agrees with reason and is conducive to the good and benefit of one and all, then accept it and live up to it."

—BUDDHA

SCRIPTURE

Jesus was very insistent. "I want you to understand this. God gave you minds to inquire, and he'll reward your using them. You were meant to seek; therefore, you will finally find. Knock at God's door, and God will open it to you. Ever so slowly, whoever asks *will* receive, whoever seeks *will* find, whoever knocks *will* be invited in. Would any good father give his child a snake when the child asked for a fish, or a scorpion instead of an egg? Well, if fathers who are imperfect know how to deal lovingly with their children, why would our Father in heaven deny them what he created them to seek?"

—LUKE 11:9–13

CLOSING

> Great Friend,
> let my search go on
> as long as
> my breathing does.
> Amen.

Spiritlessness

Quiet my mind. Open my heart. Quicken my soul.

PRESENCE

> Great Friend,
> I'd like to be reminded, often,
> that apathy
> is not the most dramatic
> form of suicide.
> Just the most common.
> Amen.

GRACE

> Father, never let me lose my zest for living.

PSALM

> "Oh, ho! I know your withered hearts so
> well!
> I know that you are neither hot nor cold.
> How I wish you were one or the other:
> fiery in your hatred or icy in your anger
> at me and all I'd hoped for you.
> But your indifference and disdain are so te-
> dious to me
> I want to vomit you out of my mouth."
> —REVELATION 3:15–16

117

HYMN

This little light of mine
I'm going to let it shine
Oh, this little light of mine
I'm going to let it shine
This little light of mine
I'm going to let it shine
Let it shine, let it shine, let it shine!

Ev'ry where I go
I'm going to let it shine.
Oh, ev'ry where I go
I'm going to let it shine.
Ev'ry where I go
I'm going to let it shine
Let it shine, let it shine, let it shine!

Out in the lonely dark
I'm going to let it shine.
Oh, out in the lonely dark
I'm going to let it shine.
Out in the lonely dark
I'm going to let it shine.
Let it shine, let it shine, let it shine!

—TRADITIONAL SPIRITUAL

READING

In the world it is called Tolerance, but in hell it is called Despair, the sin that believes in nothing, cares for nothing, seeks to know nothing, interferes with nothing, enjoys nothing, hates nothing, finds purpose in nothing, lives for nothing, and remains alive because there is nothing for which it will die.

—DOROTHY SAYERS

SCRIPTURE

Jesus told them, "I want you really to hear this: Whoever accepts what I'm saying and the Father who bids me say it *has* eternal life—not just down the line 'sometime' but *right now!* No need for a judgment. They're already home free and clear! The time is already here when even the long-dead have literally come *alive* again. The Father who is the source of *all* life has made his Son a wellspring of abundant life. [And if you have that life, it surely ought to *show*.]"

—JOHN 5:24–26

CLOSING

Great Friend,
make those I know and love
look at the way I live,
and make them wonder
where all that life comes from.
Amen.

Delayed Gratification

Quiet my mind. Open my heart. Quicken my soul.

PRESENCE

> Great Friend,
> I need reminding that,
> since I didn't exist at the time,
> I did nothing to deserve
> even being here—
> much less special treatment.
> Amen.

GRACE

> Father, help me be grateful just for making
>   the cut.

PSALM

> Lord, there is no way I could out-argue you.
> But at least I can *question* your judgments.
> (Isn't that why you gave me a critical mind?)
> Why do the unprincipled end up at the top?
> Don't tell me crime really doesn't pay.
> You seem to care for them like a fussy gar-
>   dener,
> and they have pious things to say about
>   you—

that are hollow as dried-up coconuts.
And me? I try my best, day after day.
I'd really like *something* to show for it.

—JEREMIAH 12:1–4

HYMN

Why should I feel discouraged?
Why should the shadows come?
Why should my heart be lonely
And long for heavenly home,
When Jesus is my portion?
My constant friend is he.
His eye is on the sparrow,
And I know he watches me.

I sing because I'm happy!
I sing because I'm free!
For his eye is on the sparrow,
And I know he watches me.

—TRADITIONAL SPIRITUAL

READING

To laugh often and much; To win the respect of intelligent people and the affection of children; To earn appreciation of honest critics and endure betrayal of false friends; To appreciate beauty, to find the best in others; To leave the world a bit better, whether by a healthy child, a garden patch, or a redeemed social condition; To know even one life has breathed easier because you have lived. This is to have succeeded.

—RALPH WALDO EMERSON

SCRIPTURE

Jesus told them, "Let's say you have a paid servant who's been out plowing all day or tending the sheep. So when he comes in at the end of the day, do you rush to the door and fuss over him and say, 'Oh, *please*, sit down and let me wait on you after all you've done for me.' Would any of you expect that? More likely you'd say, 'Dinner ready yet?' And only after the master is finished do the servants get their meal. It's very *nice* if the master remembers to thank them, but have they done anything to *deserve* that? As long as they get a fair wage and three meals a day for doing what they're asked to do? Isn't it that way with you and our Father? Wouldn't it be honest to say, 'I'm only doing what's right. I'm really just grateful for the chance to make a living—just to be alive'"?

—Luke 17:7–10

CLOSING

> Great Friend,
> this is a tough one,
> because I truly do
> like to see concrete rewards,
> early and often.
> Amen.

Hoarding Oneself

Quiet my mind. Open my heart. Quicken my soul.

PRESENCE

> Great Friend,
> your Son's example simply hasn't left us the
>   option
> of keeping much in reserve,
> or being shy,
> or holding back.
> Amen.

GRACE

> Father, let me not be stingy with my self.

PSALM

> God asks that we call a thing by its accurate
>   name.
> A fool is a fool, not "ill-advised and mis-
>   guided,"
> and a crook's a crook, not an "entrepreneur,"
> And a cheat's a cheat, not "a resourceful fox."
> A miser's a tightwad, not "shrewdly rich."
> They are an insult to God, those minds and
>   hearts
> and hands and pockets, sewed up so tight,

lest the lonely and needy worm their way in
and upset unbothered selfishness.

—Isaiah 32:5–8

HYMN

My candle burns at both ends;
It will not last the night;
But ah, my foes, and oh, my friends—
It gives a lovely light.

—Edna St. Vincent Millay

READING

Most people live, whether physically, intellectually, or morally, in a very restricted circle of their being. They make use of a very small portion of their possible consciousness, and of their soul's resources in general, much like a man who, out of his whole bodily organism, should get into the habit of using and moving only his little finger. Great emergencies and crises show us how much greater our vital resources are than we had supposed.

—William James

SCRIPTURE

"Don't be small-souled in judging others if you hope for mercy yourself. Stretch your heart, large enough to forgive, as you hope God will forgive. Don't be a pinchpenny. Share yourself openhandedly, and you'll receive full measure, dumped into your lap, pressed down, shaken together, and running over—more than you can hold. God will use the same measure for you as you use for others."

—Luke 6:37–38

CLOSING

Great Friend,
let me not dribble out my one life
in nickels and dimes.
Amen.

Dying to Live

Quiet my mind. Open my heart. Quicken my soul.

PRESENCE

> Great Friend,
> if I'm uneasy with paradox,
> I can never be at home
> with you, for whom
> every truth
> must have
> its irritating inconsistency.
> Amen.

GRACE

> Father, remind me that dying is what the living do.

PSALM

> And who may abide the day of his coming?
> Who will dare to stand when the Lord appears?
> For his very presence is a white-hot blaze,
> like a refiner's fire that purges impurities,
> skimming silver and gold from the worthless muck.

God's Own will burn away unworthiness
and make us worthy vessels to contain his
   life.

—MALACHI 3:2–4

HYMN

Way down yonder in the graveyard walk
   I thank God I'm free at last.
Me and my Jesus going to meet and talk
   I thank God I'm free at last.
On my knees when the light pass'd by
   I thank God I'm free at last.
Tho't my soul would rise and fly
   I thank God I'm free at last.
Some of these mornings, bright and fair
   I thank God I'm free at last
Goin' meet King Jesus in the air
   I thank God I'm free at last.
Free at last, free at last
   I thank God I'm free at last
Free at last, free at last
   I thank God Almighty I'm free at last!

—TRADITIONAL SPIRITUAL

READING

Adversity is a severe instructor, set over us by one who
knows us better than we do ourselves, as he loves us better,
too. He that wrestles with us strengthens our nerves and
sharpens our skill. Our antagonist is our helper. This conflict
with difficulty makes us acquainted with our object, and
compels us to consider it in all its relations. It will not suffer
us to be superficial.

—EDMUND BURKE

SCRIPTURE

Jesus called the crowd to join the apostles, because this wasn't just for the few. "If you want to count yourself one of mine," he told them, "you have to leave your selfishness behind, pick up your cross, and watch the way I carry mine. Do it with dignity. Conquer by yielding. If you want to win, surrender pretensions and take the place God finds you worthy of. Your true self will find you, once you stop making yourself the sole object of your searching. If you give up everything to reach the top (which is *not* your place anyway), what do you have left worth having when there's no 'you'?"

—MARK 8:34–37

CLOSING

Great Friend,
some say
unwelcome challenge
expresses your deepest gratitude.
That *can't* really be true.
Can it?
Really?
Amen.

The Big Yearning

Quiet my mind. Open my heart. Quicken my soul.

PRESENCE

> Great Friend,
> sometimes
> when I open the narrow focus
> of my everyday awareness
> to the Really Real,
> you overwhelm me.
> Amen.

GRACE

> Father, don't let me settle for a secure, shriv-
> eled life.

PSALM 42

> Just as a deer searches for water,
> my soul is thirsty for "a place to call home,"
> something to fill my God-sized emptiness.
> This vague uneasiness needs a place to rest,
> a feeling that all the pieces make sense.
> When I was small, that feeling meant Mom,
> whose arms made everything right again.
> Then I found that need pointed to you.

I long to get that childlike wholeness back.
Lord, my emptiness is waiting for you.

HYMN

My life is like a faded leaf,
My harvest dwindled to a husk,
Truly my life is void and brief
And tedious in the barren dusk;
My life is like a frozen thing,
No bud nor greenness can I see:
Yet rise it shall—the sap of spring,
O Jesus, rise in me.

—CHRISTINA ROSSETTI

READING

God is infinite and without end, but the soul's desire is an abyss which cannot be filled except by a Good which is infinite; and the more ardently the soul longeth after God, the more she *wills* to long after him; for God is a Good without drawback, and a well of living water without bottom, and the soul is made in the image of God, and therefore it is created to know and love God.

—JOHANNES TAULER

SCRIPTURE

As Jesus sat at the well waiting for his men to return, a woman came to draw water—at a time the other women wouldn't be there. "Give me a drink," he asked.

She frowned at him: "A Jew? Did you notice I'm a Samaritan dog?" (A pious Jew would never use a Samaritan cup or bowl.)

Jesus answered, "If you knew who I really am and how bountiful God is, you'd be asking *me* to give *you* waters that keep you forever alive."

She cocked an eye at him. "Stranger, you don't even have a bucket, and the well is deep. Where would you get this life-giving water?"

Jesus smiled. "Whoever drinks from this well here will get thirsty again before long. But those who drink the water I offer will never be thirsty again. Never. It will gush up in an endless torrent from within the soul."

—JOHN 4:4–26

CLOSING

Great Friend,
slake my thirst,
but let me keep my thirsting.
Amen.

Indebtedness

Quiet my mind. Open my heart. Quicken my soul.

PRESENCE

> Great Friend,
> what can I offer you
> to repay your kindness,
> when all I have to give
> has been your gift to me?
> Amen.

GRACE

> Father, keep me astonished at my good for-
> tune.

PSALM

> My soul exults in thanks to God,
> and my heart rejoices in him, my savior,
> for he actually *cares* for someone as lowly
> as I!
> Who could deny how blessed I am,
> because he's done great things—for *me*.
> His name has been holy since before there
> was time,
> and he pours out his mercy on those who
> revere him.

He's scattered the proud and their plans
and raised up the lonely, the hungry, the
nobodies.

—LUKE 1:46–52

HYMN

Now thank we all our God, with hearts and
hands and voices,
Who wondrous things has done, in whom
this world rejoices;
Who from our mothers' arms has blessed us
on our way
With countless gifts of love, and still is ours
today.

Oh, may this bounteous God through all our
life be near us,
With ever joyful hearts and blessèd peace to
cheer us;
And keep us in his grace, and guide us when
perplexed;
And free us from all ills, in this world and
the next!

All praise and thanks to God the Father now
be given;
The Son and he who reigns with them in
highest heaven;
The one eternal God, whom earth and heaven
adore;
For thus it was, is now, and shall be ever-
more.

—ATTRIBUTED TO MARTIN RINKART

READING

In relation to God, we are like a thief who has burgled the house of a kindly householder and been allowed to keep some of the gold. In the eyes of the lawful owner this gold is gift; In the eyes of the burglar it is theft. He must give it back. It is the same with our existence. We have stolen a little of God's being to make it ours. God made us a gift of it. But we have stolen it. We must return it.

—Simone Weil

SCRIPTURE

Jesus entered a town on the Samaria-Galilee border and encountered ten men, all of them lepers. They cringed at a distance, but nonetheless they shouted to him, "Jesus! Master! Pity us!"

"Yes. I do," Jesus said. "Now, go show yourselves to the priests."

While they were on their way, they were suddenly made clean!

One of them looked at his own arms and legs, unable to believe his eyes, and turned back, running breathlessly back to Jesus, shouting his gratitude to God. He threw himself face down into the dirt at Jesus' feet, choking out his thanks. Oddly, he was a despised Samaritan.

Jesus looked down at him and said, quietly, "Weren't there ten? Where are the other nine? The only thankful one is this foreigner?" he smiled at the man and brushed back his forelock. "Go, friend. Your faith made you well."

—Luke 17:11–19

CLOSING

Great Friend,
I did nothing

to deserve an invitation.
Never let me complain
about the accommodations.
Amen.

Puzzlements

Quiet my mind. Open my heart. Quicken my soul.

PRESENCE

> Great Friend,
> you gave me a mind
> to discover you,
> not to outwit you,
> nor to second guess you,
> much less to take your place.
> Amen.

GRACE

> Father, you are as hard to nail down as mercury.

PSALM

> How bottomless are your richness and wis-
> dom!
> Who could question your judgments or deci-
> pher your ways?
> Who can fathom the mind of God?
> Would even a fool dare offer God advice?
> Everything comes from him, through him,
> for him.
> God forever distant—and yet here at my side!
> —ROMANS 11:33–36

HYMN

What art thou, then, my God?
Most distant, yet most caring,
most potent, most gentle;
most merciful and most just;
most unapproachable, most present;
most lovely and most strong,
so firm yet so elusive,
never then, always now.
And what have I now said, my God, my life,
    my holy joy?
Or what says anyone who speaks of you?
Yet woe to those who keep silent about
    you,
when so many babble on and capture noth-
    ing.

—AUGUSTINE OF HIPPO

READING

In the beginning, God created the earth, and he looked upon it in His cosmic loneliness.

And God said, "Let Us make living creatures out of mud, so the mud can see what We have done." And God created every living creature that now moveth, and one was man. Mud as man alone could speak. God leaned close as mud as man sat, looked around, and spoke. Man blinked. "What is the purpose of all this?" he asked politely.

"Everything must have a purpose?" asked God.

"Certainly," said man.

"Then I leave it to you to think of one for all this," said God.

And He went away.

—KURT VONNEGUT, JR.

SCRIPTURE

Jesus spoke again to the self-righteous Pharisees. "I am the light of the world. I've come so you needn't keep stumbling around in the darkness."

The Pharisees sniffed. "Oh, really? Assertions without evidence prove nothing. We're supposed to believe you—as the sole witness to this drivel?"

"No," Jesus answered, "but testifying for myself doesn't make me automatically untrustworthy, because I know where I've been and where I'm going. You pass judgment as if humans see and understand everything that is. But if the Law requires two witnesses, I'm not alone. The Father who sent me testifies to me, too. Two witnesses: the Father and I."

—JOHN 8:12–18

CLOSING

Great Friend,
let me rejoice in the quest
without demanding
to "arrive."
Amen.

Presence

Quiet my mind. Open my heart. Quicken my soul.

PRESENCE

> Great Friend,
> you are the aliveness
> who pulses in stars and starfish,
> in daisies and dolphins,
> and in me.
> Amen.

GRACE

> Father, help me accept that your greatness
> values my smallness.

PSALM

> Solomon prayed at the dedication of the
> Temple:
> "Oh, God, no matter how enormous it seems
> to us,
> can you confine your immeasurable greatness
> into this space?
> You, whom the boundless universe cannot
> contain?
> How can this Temple we have built be large
> enough?

Take pity on the boldness of my prayer:
Watch over this Temple day and night.
You've promised you would meet us in this
     place,
so hear us when we turn this way and pray.
And in your heaven beyond our swiftest
     thoughts
hear our hearts' petitions and forgive."
                              —2 CHRONICLES 6:18–21

HYMN

All are but parts of one stupendous whole,
Whose body Nature is, and God the soul;
That, chang'd through all, and yet in all the
     same,
Great in the earth, as in th' ethereal frame,
Warms in the sun, refreshes in the breeze,
Glows in the stars, and blossoms in the trees,
Lives through all life, extends through all
     extent,
Spreads undivided, operates unspent,
Breathes in our soul, informs our mortal part,
As full, as perfect, in a hair as heart;
As full, as perfect, in vile man that mourns,
As the rapt seraph that adores and burns;
To him no high, no low, no great, no small;
He fills, he bounds, connects, and equals all.
                              —ALEXANDER POPE

READING

The sacred fire is well concealed in the wood like a child in
the womb of the mother. The Soul is contained in the body as
the fire is contained and concealed in the wood. Fire breaks
forth and takes shape in accordance with the thing burning. It is now the flame of a lamp, now a furnace and now a

forest fire, according as to where it is manifested. The fire by itself is one and the same. So also, the Soul though manifold in embodiment, is the same as that in which it abides for the time being.

—UPANISHADS

SCRIPTURE

Jesus said to them, "And let me tell you something you can depend on. Whenever even just two of you on earth have a union of hearts and pray for what you want, have no doubt whatever that my Father hears you. Because whenever two or three come together in my name, I am there with them. Count on it."

—MATTHEW 18:19–20

CLOSING

Great Friend,
I'm not worthy
that you should come into my soul.
But only say the word,
and my own worth doesn't matter.
Amen.

Hangin' In There

Quiet my mind. Open my heart. Quicken my soul.

PRESENCE

> Great Friend,
> when I truly believe
> that it is you who ask me,
> how can I still believe
> I can't?
> Amen.

GRACE

> Father, help me see that anything precious
> comes at a price.

PSALM

> When the going gets tough, the tough get
> going.
> A true soldier does the job,
> doing what's asked, despite the boredom.
> A runner never attains the prize
> by merely outwitting the rules.
> No honest farmer expects a harvest
> without the day-to-day donkey work.
> Mull that over, and the Lord (who knows)
> will help you grasp "the way things are."
>
> —2 Timothy 2:3–7

HYMN

Success is counted sweetest
By those who ne'er succeed.
To comprehend a nectar
Requires sorest need.
Not one of all the purple Host
Who took the Flag today
Can tell the definition
So clear of Victory
As he defeated—dying—
On whose forbidden ear
The distant strains of triumph
Burst agonized and clear!

—EMILY DICKINSON

READING

The harder the conflict, the more glorious the triumph. What we obtain too cheap, we esteem too lightly; it is dearness only that gives everything its value. I love the man that can smile in trouble, that can gather strength from distress and grow brave by reflection. 'Tis the business of little minds to shrink; but he whose heart is firm, and whose conscience approves his conduct, will pursue his principles unto death.

—THOMAS PAINE

SCRIPTURE

The high priest stood up in front of all the elders and sneered at Jesus, "*Well?* Have you nothing to say to these accusations they bring against you?"

But Jesus refused to answer and stood silent.

Becoming furious, the high priest again demanded, "*Are you the Messiah, the Son of God?*"

Jesus looked straight into the high priest's eyes and said between his teeth, "I *AM!* And one day you'll see the Son of Man come on the clouds of heaven!"

The high priest was so incensed he could hardly get breath to shriek. He tore his robes according to ritual. "Who needs witnesses?" he cried. "He's condemned out of his own mouth! Hear the *blasphemy!*" He looked wildly around at his fellow judges. "What's your verdict, my brothers?"

The verdict was unanimous: Guilty. Death.

Some priests spat in Jesus' face. They blindfolded him and smacked him with the backs of their hands. "Hah!" some cried. "Guess who hit you!"

And the guards, whipping and slapping him, led him away.

—MARK 14:60–65

CLOSING

Great Friend,
you've been there.
You understand.
Help me to understand.
Amen.

You're Connected

Quiet my mind. Open my heart. Quicken my soul.

PRESENCE

> Great Friend,
> help me grasp and feel
> the real union I share
> with all those who inhabit this earth,
> with all those who have ever lived,
> and with the Three of you.
> Amen.

GRACE

> Father, let me accept this new life surging in
> me—in us.

PSALM

> Christ is like a single body, with many parts,
> but still one, no matter how dissimilar the
> parts.
> If we're one, then it's wrong to keep using
> the old labels like *Jew* or *Gentile*,
> *slave or free, male or female.*
> The eye can't say to the hand, "Who needs
> you?"
> We simply can't get along divided.

145

We *need* even the unlearned parts,
the un-beautiful parts, the persnickety parts.
No matter what anyone thinks of you—
even you yourself—God thinks you matter.
                    —I CORINTHIANS 12:12–14, 21–25

HYMN

No man is an island, entire of itself;
every man is a piece of the continent, a part
    of the main.
If a clod be washed away by the sea, Europe
    is the less,
as well as if a promontory were,
as well as if a manor of thy friend's or of
    thine own were.
Any man's death diminishes me, because I am
    involved in mankind,
and therefore never send to know for whom
    the bell tolls;
it tolls for thee.

                            — JOHN DONNE

READING

I paused to listen to the silence. My breath, crystallized
as it passed my cheeks, drifted on a breeze gentler than a
whisper. The wind vane pointed toward the South Pole. . . .
The day was dying, the night was being born but with great
peace. Here were the imponderable processes and forces of
the cosmos, harmonious and soundless. Harmony, that was it!
That was what came out of the silence—a gentle rhythm, the
strain of a perfect chord, the music of the spheres, perhaps. It
was enough to catch that rhythm, momentarily to be myself a
part of it. In that instant I could feel no doubt of man's oneness with the universe. The conviction came that that rhythm
was too orderly, too harmonious, too perfect to be a product

of blind chance that, therefore, there must be purpose in the whole and that man was part of that whole and not an accidental offshoot. It was a feeling that transcended reason; that went to the heart of a man's despair and found it groundless. . . . For those who seek it, there is inexhaustible evidence of an all-pervading intelligence. Man is not alone.

—ADMIRAL RICHARD E. BYRD

SCRIPTURE

Jesus said, "I am the vine, and my Father works the vineyard. He hacks off every branch in me that refuses to bear fruit. But he also prunes back—sometimes harshly—every branch that does bear good grapes so that it can yield even more bountifully. Your accepting what I've told you has done that. Cling in union to me, and I will grasp you into myself. A branch can't bear fruit all alone; it fruits only if it remains grafted into the vine. In the same way, you will bear fruit for our Father only as you remain joined into me."

—JOHN 15:1–4

CLOSING

Great Friend,
the most liberating discovery
is that,
no matter what my feelings,
I am never, ever
truly alone.
Amen.

What Counts

Quiet my mind. Open my heart. Quicken my soul.

PRESENCE

> Great Friend,
> I'm easily distracted,
> diverted, disturbed.
> Keep your guiding hand
> on my shoulder.
> Amen.

GRACE

> Father, help me to keep focused on what really matters.

PSALM

> When we let Christ's Spirit invade our souls,
> She makes a new kind of life grow within us:
> honest affection for those we despised,
> exuberance for living, and serenity of heart,
> smiling endurance of what we thought unbearable,
> kindness and compassion for the weak and fearful,
> a firm belief in the inner goodness of people,

and the confidence to stand for the truth.
No law ever written could make that happen.

—GALATIANS 5:22–26

HYMN

The pure, the bright, the beautiful
that stirred our hearts in youth,
The impulses to wordless prayer,
The streams of love and truth,
The longing after something lost,
The spirit's longing cry,
The striving after better hopes—
These things can never die.

The timid hand stretched forth to aid
A brother in his need;
A kindly word in grief's dark hour
That proves a friend indeed;
The plea for mercy softly breathed,
When justice threatens high,
The sorrow of a contrite heart—
These things shall never die.

—CHARLES DICKENS

READING

Don't aim at success—the more you aim at it and make it a target, the more you are going to miss it. For success, like happiness, cannot be pursued; it must result, and it only does so as the unintended side effect of one's personal dedication to a cause greater than oneself or as the by-product of one's surrender to a person other than oneself. Happiness must happen, and the same holds for success: you have to let it happen by not caring about it. Listen to what your conscience commands you to do and go on to carry it out to the best of your knowledge. Then you will live to see that in the long-run—in the long-run, I say!—success will follow you precisely because you had forgotten to think about it.

—Viktor Frankl

SCRIPTURE

Jesus said, "If only I could make you see this. If only I could make you *relax* and trust God. Fret, fuss, stew! How can I guarantee my family will have enough to eat and drink? And what about clothes and all the other bills? Isn't that what the world *insists* you worry about? Your Father in heaven knows you need all those things. Stop fretting about what you're missing. If you fret, you'll miss out on *life*! Try to discern what God's drawing you to do and become, right now, and God will find a way to take care of all that you think is more important than the life it supports. And don't imagine all the things that will go wrong tomorrow! The important task is preparing the self who has to face *whatever* tomorrow brings."

—Matthew 6:31–34

CLOSING

Great Friend,
give me the confidence
to surrender myself
to you.
Amen.

Hope

Quiet my mind. Open my heart. Quicken my soul.

PRESENCE

> Great Friend,
> for your own reasons
> you hold certitude from us.
> Help us be content, then,
> with faith, hope, and love.
> Amen.

GRACE

> Father, just help me feel your hand as I
> fumble in the dark.

PSALM 33

> The Lord is so watchful for those who value
> him,
> those who count on his loving sustenance.
> In his hands they are safe even from death,
> no matter how dire or lean the times.
> We put our hope where it belongs, in the
> Lord,
> our unfailing protector and our assurance
> against fear.

Who could tremble or sulk or moan with
     such a Friend?
He has shared with us his holy name!
Help us to feel your love, O Lord,
as we root all our hopes in you.

HYMN

Soft as the voice of an angel,
Breathing a lesson unheard,
Hope with a gentle persuasion
Whispers her comforting word:
Wait till the darkness is over,
Wait till the tempest is done,
Hope for the sunshine tomorrow,
After the shower is gone.
     Whispering hope, oh, how welcome thy
          voice,
     Making my heart in its sorrow rejoice.
Hope, as an anchor so steadfast,
Rends the dark veil for the soul,
Whither the Master has entered,
Robbing the grave of its goal;
Come then, oh, come, glad fruition,
Come to my sad weary heart;
Come, O Thou blest hope of glory,
Never, oh, never depart.
     Whispering hope, oh, how welcome thy
          voice,
     Making my heart in its sorrow rejoice.
                              —Septimus Winner

READING

Hope is a state of mind, not of the world. . . . Either we
have hope or we don't; it is a dimension of the soul, and it is

not essentially dependent on some particular observation of the world or estimate of the situation. Hope is not prophecy. It is an orientation of the spirit, an orientation of the heart; it transcends the world that is immediately experienced, and is anchored somewhere beyond its horizons. . . . Hope, in this deep and powerful sense, is not the same as joy that things are going well, or willingness to invest in enterprises that are obviously heading for success, but rather an ability to work for something because it is good, not just because it stands a chance to succeed. The more propitious the situation in which we demonstrate hope, the deeper the hope is. Hope is definitely not the same thing as optimism. It is not the conviction that something will turn out well, but the certainty that something makes sense, regardless of how it turns out.

—Vaclav Havel

SCRIPTURE

After he'd joined them on the road to Emmaus, Jesus asked his two new companions why they were so mournful. They wondered if he'd heard of the crushing events in Jerusalem that weekend, and when he pretended ignorance, they told him. "It's about what happened to Jesus of Nazareth. A prophet who clearly spoke God's own truth. Our chief priests turned him over to the governor and got him crucified. We'd hoped . . . we'd been *sure* he was the one to set us free! That was three days ago. And now . . . now some women have us completely befuddled with talk that he's risen. And jabbering about an angel. Can you believe that? Some of our people went, and the tomb *was* empty, but . . . I mean . . . "

Then Jesus said, "Ah, how stubborn-headed. Didn't the prophets show that the One-to-Come *had* to suffer in order to share his glory?" And he went through all the scriptures, showing them God's promises, fulfilled that very weekend!

—Luke 24:19–27

CLOSING

Great Friend,
you are the anchor
that keeps us safe.
Amen.

Paradoxes

Quiet my mind. Open my heart. Quicken my soul.

PRESENCE

> Great Friend,
> something nearly untamable in me
> wants—perversely—to tame you.
> Amen.

GRACE

> Father, let me rest comfortably with your
>   unwillingness to be captured.

PSALM

> To become the total fool, keep abreast of
>   trends,
> what "everybody" knows and "everybody"
>   does.
> That's now deemed by most as "thinking for
>   yourself,"
> If you're truly wise, you'll look the fool to
>   them,
> because God's wisdom looks like nonsense to
>   the shallow—
> while their profundities are spider webs to
>   him.

The Truth is far too subtle to be captured in
    a box
or comfortably trapped in a whole library
    of books.
—1 Corinthians 3:18–21

HYMN

Batter my heart, three-person'd God ; for you
As yet but knock ; breathe, shine, and seek
    to mend ;
That I may rise, and stand, o'erthrow me,
    and bend
Your force, to break, blow, burn, and make
    me new.
I, like an usurp'd town, to another due,
Labour to admit you, but O, to no end.
Reason, your viceroy in me, me should de-
    fend,
But is captived, and proves weak or untrue.
Yet dearly I love you, and would be loved
    fain,
But am betroth'd unto your enemy ;
Divorce me, untie, or break that knot again,
Take me to you, imprison me, for I,
Except you enthrall me, never shall be free,
Nor ever chaste, except you ravish me.
—John Donne

READING

Anxiety is secretive. He does not trust anyone, not even his friends, Worry, Terror, Doubt, and Panic. He has a way of glombing onto your skin like smog, and then you feel unclean. He likes to visit me late at night when I am alone and exhausted. I have never slept with him but he kissed me on the forehead once, and I had a headache for two years. He is sure a nuisance to get out of the house, he has no respect for locks or curtains or doors. I speak from experience. It takes cunning to get rid of him, a combination of anger, humor, and self-respect. A bath helps too. He does not like to get wet. As a last resort, if you are not near a bathtub, wet your face with tears.

—J. RUTH GENDLER

SCRIPTURE

When they'd reached the comparative security of Capernaum, Jesus asked his men, "What were you arguing about on the road?" They fumbled and tried to avoid answering, like called-on schoolboys, because they'd been asking about which one of them Jesus favored most, who would be the greatest of them when his kingdom began. Jesus sighed and shook his head, signaling them to sit down around him. "Whoever wants to take the first place should come to the end of the line. With me. Become everybody's servant." There was a child standing there, and Jesus lifted him onto his lap, and the boy leaned his head against Jesus' chest, sucking his thumb.

"Here's the answer to 'who's greatest,'" he smiled. "Unless you change and become like this child, you'll never even recognize the *entrance* to the kingdom. The greatest is whoever is this humble, this open to wonder, this nonjudgmental. And whoever values a child like this for me, welcomes me."

—MARK 9:33–37; MATTHEW 18:1–5

CLOSING

Great Friend,
help me accept your habit
of turning things upside down
just when I have them
"figured out."
Amen.

Having a Why

Quiet my mind. Open my heart. Quicken my soul.

PRESENCE

Great Friend,
just as you've created me
and called me,
continue to sustain me.
Amen.

GRACE

Father, keep firm my conviction of your ap-
proval.

PSALM

I never want to be accused of being fickle,
of talking out of both sides of my mouth,
of flipping from yes to no when it's more
    convenient.
I want to be as true to my word as God is
    to his.
The Jesus we cling to is no weaseling Maybe.
Jesus is a strong, clean, in-your-face Yes!
to all of God's promises. Count on that.

—2 Corinthians 1:17–22

158

HYMN

Anyone can fight the battle of just one day.
It is when you and I add the burdens of those
  two awful eternities
Yesterday and Tomorrow that we break
  down.
It is not the experience of Today that drives
  a person mad,
It is the remorse or bitterness of something
  which happened Yesterday
and the dread of what Tomorrow may bring.
Let us, therefore, Live but one day at a time.

—Author Unknown

READING

This uniqueness and singleness which distinguishes each
individual and gives a meaning to his existence has a bearing
on creative work as much as it does on human love. When
the impossibility of replacing a person is realized, it allows the
responsibility which a man has for his existence and its con-
tinuance to appear in all its magnitude. A man who becomes
conscious of the responsibility he bears toward a human being
who affectionately waits for him, or to an unfinished work,
will never be able to throw away his life. He knows the "why"
for his existence, and will be able to bear almost any "how."

—Viktor Frankl

SCRIPTURE

Jesus began to speak more openly with his disciples. "The
Son of Man," he said, "must soon face an ordeal. The leaders
and priests and teachers of the Law are getting ready to reject
me publicly. I'm going to be put to death. But be sure of this,
three days later I will come back into life."

Peter was irate. He took Jesus by the elbow and led him away from the others. "Master," he growled, "stop talking like that! I won't allow it!"

But Jesus was genuinely furious. "Get out of my way, you devil! You don't know what you're talking about again. You haven't the slightest idea what God wants of me!"

—MATTHEW 16:21–23

CLOSING

Great Friend,
what you ask
is often unnerving,
but it's far better
than aimless blundering about.
Amen.

Shalom

Quiet my mind. Open my heart. Quicken my soul.

PRESENCE

> Great Friend,
> I ask not for the peace
> of the undisturbed
> but the peace
> of the tightrope walker.
> Amen.

GRACE

> Father, my trust in your truth gives me hope.

PSALM

> If you want God to be glad that he invited
>   you,
> speak nothing hurtful, turn gossip aside,
> hold the hearts of your neighbors holy.
> Turn your back on anything bitter or small,
> and make peace the ultimate quest of your
>   soul.
> Who can harm you if your intentions are
>   worthy?
> Don't worry. You have nothing to fear.
> But be ready at a moment's notice to explain

the Cause of your tranquility and joy.
And if you must suffer, suffer for doing
what's right.
—1 PETER 3:10–17

HYMN

Peace is not the product of terror or fear.
Peace is not the silence of cemeteries.
Peace is not the silent result of violent repres-
sion.
Peace is the generous, tranquil contribution
of all to the good of all.
Peace is dynamism. Peace is generosity.
It is right and it is duty.
—OSCAR ROMERO

READING

One has to abandon altogether the search for security, and reach out with both arms to the risk of living. One has to court doubt and darkness as the cost of knowing. One needs a will stubborn in conflict, but apt always to total acceptance of every consequence of living and dying.
—MORRIS L. WEST

SCRIPTURE

To the women's astonishment, they saw an angel sitting in the doorway of tomb, as bright as lightning. "You must not be afraid," the angel said. "Yes, I know. You came looking for Jesus who was crucified. But he's not here! He's *alive* again! Just as he promised. Come. Don't be afraid. Look where you saw them lay his body. See?"
The women looked and saw the place was empty.

"Go quickly now and tell the others. He's been raised from death and has gone ahead to Galilee. Remember what I've told you. Fear nothing!"

The women turned back toward the city, trying to keep their hearts clutched in their chests, when suddenly there he was! Jesus! Smiling, holding out his welcoming hands: "Peace," he said. "Peace! Peace!"

They fell to the ground and grasped at his feet, trying to comprehend so much impossibility all at once.

"Don't be afraid," Jesus told them. "You have no need ever to be afraid again. Go tell the others I will meet them, too."

—MATTHEW 28:3, 5–10

CLOSING

> Great Friend,
> grant me
> the serenity
> to accept the things I cannot change,
> the courage
> to change the things I can,
> and the wisdom
> to know the difference.
> Amen.

Ways to Use This Book

The primary rule for prayer helpers, printed or human, is to know when to get out of the way. We do-gooders have to keep reminding ourselves we are, indeed, merely matchmakers. We bring the two parties together and tease them into awareness of each other—though God is already aware and more. Then we have to slip (hopefully unnoticed) out of the picture and trust that the two principals have an instinct about what to do next. This segment of the book has been told to "step to the rear" so that it won't intrude on people who have picked up the book just to find ways to withdraw themselves from the uproar and discover nonintrusive suggestions for a path along which a person-to-Person connection to God might *begin*.

But there are other situations where the book might be useful. For example, in group a few suggestions might be helpful if the person delegated to "come up with something" is inexperienced.

LEADING A PRAYER CLASS
OR AN ADULT PRAYER GROUP

It's probably worthwhile, before you introduce praying at all, to talk about what it "requires" if your invitation is to have even a chance of being effective.

First, a *place*—somewhere you aren't likely to be intruded upon. Turn off the cell phone; dare to brave the silence and solitude that invites God to join you. (If your chapel isn't large enough for the class or is unavailable, push back the chairs and sit on the floor—folks spaced at some distance from one another so you're not distracted by others' breathing and belly gurgles.)

Second, you need to choose a *posture*, foolish as that sounds. If you are totally comfortable, you're bound to fall asleep. Some can achieve a yoga lotus; most can't. But if you sit on the floor with your back to a wall or in a chair, feet crossed and comfortable, hands open and receptive on your knees, you will be comfortable without inviting a nap. Relax—which is not as easy as one might think. Even when we're sprawled, there's an inner guard always intensely aware of any threat of trespass. It's difficult for even God to penetrate our defenses if we're always ready to jerk our dukes up.

Third, you need a *focus* to come back to when you're distracted. And you will be distracted by cricks in your neck or suddenly remembering you forgot to call Eddie. Resolve that, at least for a few minutes, the earth will keep on spinning without your awareness and control. You can focus on your breathing—deep, long breaths (this is almost impossible to teach non-smokers!), being in peace, close-to-but-not-all-the-way to sleep. Or you can focus on a physical object—a candle, an orange, a stone, a crucifix. Or choose a repeated mantra like "God, my Friend, somehow you're alive in me," or the "hook" of an idea from the book's prayer-starters that clings like a burr in your mind.

Then, in a first meeting, explain what the session is going to entail:

> *I'm going to ask you first to relax. Rotate your head around and let all the tension and "in chargeness" drain down into your shoulders, down your arms and back, into the floor. Make a calm place inside yourself, a place where you're not the "driver," and invite God to join you there and take the wheel. Then I'll read a prayer that tries to focus that invitation to God. I'll pause and let you handle it whatever way you want. Then, if you feel*

you want to share some genuine feeling aloud, don't be afraid to speak. No more than a sentence or two. You don't have to speak because the person next to you has spoken. If fact, you don't have to speak at all. Then I'll read a very short prayer asking for a grace, like "Help me to let go, God, and let you take over," just to focus the connection. And I'll read a "psalm," a part of the scripture compressed into a kind of formalized prayer. And I'll pause again for a while, and if that's given you the urge to share a short thought, feel free. Then I'll read a poem or a hymn, and pause. Then a reading from something other than scripture, and pause. Then a reading from the Gospels, and pause.

At none of those pauses do you have to speak. The important thing isn't that you open up to the group but that you open up to God. If you do share with the group, it will help us all to know we're not the only ones trying. But God can work without us if he chooses.

Doing the above "setting-up" should probably take about fifteen minutes of demonstration and talk, at least in the first session. But even in later sessions with the same group, the leader has to take some time to "bleed out the world," to clear a path to that empty place only God can satisfy. The modern soul is hidden far more deeply within self-defensive barriers than it was when most of the great pray-ers were trying to explain how to do it.

Begin the actual prayer session by saying quietly for the group:

Quiet my mind. Open my heart. Quicken my soul.

Pause a bit to let each person ingest that. Then begin the process outlined above.

If everyone in the group has a book, you can ask others beforehand if they will read a segment, waiting for you to give them the nod when you sense the group is ready to move on.

You definitely do not have to "get through" all the prayers in each meditation in the book. Keep your antennae tuned to the body language and sounds in the room. If they're restless, move on. If they exhibit an unusual serenity, back off. Let God be God!

THE MORNING SCHOOL PUBLIC ADDRESS (PA) PRAYER

The prayers were written with a meticulous eye to avoiding insulting intelligent people—things like, "Hi there, you swingin' teens! Ready to get down and, like, *pray?*" The topics try to engage *adult* attitudes, fears, confusions. And these beset youngsters precisely because they are bewildered by adult issues for the first time. Therefore, though a word or two may be beyond this particular age group, the person in charge can always dip into the thesaurus.

Surely it would be self-defeating to use a whole segment just for a morning prayer over a PA system, but it is not too burdensome to use the Presence and Closing prayers and choose one of the Psalm, Reading, Hymn, or Scripture elements you think is likely to snag the students' curiosity. (That is the sine qua non. If you fail to puzzle listeners to attentiveness, they will not be listeners but be busy whispering, "Anybody do the math?")

Presuming the homeroom teachers have gotten them quiet, dare to leave just a few seconds of silence after each reading. You won't have all or even most of them open to the connection, but you have Jesus' word that *some* of the seed will fall on good ground.

PRAYING IN RELIGIOUS ED CLASS

The book could serve as a text or adjunct text for a formal prayer class. If so, a teacher gutsy enough to offer such a course needs no advice. However, because of the formalization and efficiency madness that threatens all genuine learning in a school, other religious ed teachers often forget that the fundamental purpose of what we do is *not* to prepare young people to appear on Mother Angelica's version of "Jeopardy." What we do is always in service to *religion*, that is, always pointing (however remotely) at that person-to-Person connection. We tend to forget that Voltaire knew immeasurably more *about* God than the Curé of Ars. But one could at least surmise that the parish priest who failed theology exams with embarrassing regularity knew *God* far more richly and intensely than the sophisticated philosopher. But sometimes our summer courses and advanced degrees skew our perceptions of our ultimate aim.

If we want *To Teach as Jesus Did*,[4] it's wise to discover how to do that, not from the mandated syllabus but from the Gospels themselves. Jesus clearly did not aim for theological thoroughness but for a radical change of heart—of attitudes and values. No matter where one teaches today, it is axiomatic that the audience we serve is more attuned to the siren songs of Madison Avenue than to the Sermon on the Mount. *But,* the God-sized hunger is still there within each student, and it behooves even religious ed teachers who expound about church history or sacraments or Christology to give over at least a class or two each semester to a session that tries to introduce students to the Subject who makes us believe the subject worth studying.

A CAUTION ON THE SCRIPTURE PASSAGES

The Psalms and Scripture passages in this book are in no way strict translations, nor are they approved by the official church for liturgical use. They are just the author's response to the scripture writers' provocations, the reactions of an

---

[4] The title of the 1972 USCCB publication on educational ministry.

eighty-year veteran to a divinely inspired Rorschach. They are what movies mean when the credits say "Inspired by an Actual Event."

With that, I have the good grace to go silent and withdraw.